LOST
TREASURES
Of the World

Ex Líbrís

Randy Manning

This edition published in the United Kingdom 1993 by MMB,
an imprint of Multimedia Books Limited,
32-34 Gordon House Road, London NW5 1LP

Editors: Richard Rosenfeld, Edward Bunting, Tony Hall, Dan Miller
Research: Arthur Butterfield, Ian Knight
Production: Hugh Allan
Design: Ruty Stopnitzki-Orbach
Picture Research: Charlotte Deane, Anne Horton

10 9 8 7 6 5 4 3 2 1

A catalogue record for this book
is available from The British Library.

ISBN 1-85375-126-X

Printed in Hong Kong

LOST
TREASURES
Of the World

Michael Groushko

MMB

Contents

Introduction

'When I first saw it I knew what it was — a reef of silver bars. I just started screaming...I kind of lost control of myself.' The speaker was young diver Andy Matrochi, one of the team that found perhaps the most exciting lost treasure located in our time, a laden Spanish galleon that sank off the cost of Florida more than 360 years ago and is now yielding gold, silver, and gems worth $450 million. The wreck was 16 years of dedication and danger in the finding and every treasure-hunter's dream come true.

But for every secret hoard the earth gives up, there is another still to be traced, from the reputed treasures of ancient conquerors to the latterday spoils of Adolf Hitler. Clues as to their whereabouts lie in misty legends and in modern bank vaults, for those with perseverance enough to track them down.

Famous examples of treasures lost and found are detailed in the following pages. Who knows, their dramatic stores may even inspire you to begin treasure hunting in a small way yourself. Remember, the past is all around us, its secrets ready to be discovered by whoever looks the hardest, and that does not just mean the professional treasure seeker with his impressive array of resources.

The advent of high technology has turned treasure hunting into big business, but without stripping it of any of its romantic appeal. For the technology can be used only when the approximate site has been located.

One aspect of treasurehunting that is changing, however, is its relationship with branches of academic study, particularly archaeology and history. No longer is it respectable, if it ever was, to strip potential sites with explosives to secure their treasure while destroying intrinsically valueless but archaeologically invaluable material. Governments are placing increasing restrictions on the granting of exploration licenses, and archaeologists and other specialists are now members of many exploration teams.

It is no part of this book's purpose to encourage the plundering of archaeological sites or the invasion of private property. Appendix II describes the law as it applies in general to treasure hunting (or, for that matter, archaeological investigation), with some further guidelines to good conduct. To those should be added one more: context — the surrounds and circumstances in which objects are found, and the spatial relationships between those objects — is all-important in modern archaeology. Expert advice should always be sought *before* disturbing a site.

To armchair and active treasure hunters, the quest holds many thrills independent of the actual find. It is only at the last stage that technology and academic expertise need come into play. Until that moment, any treasure hunter can be as alone with the secret dream as he or she wishes. Good hunting!

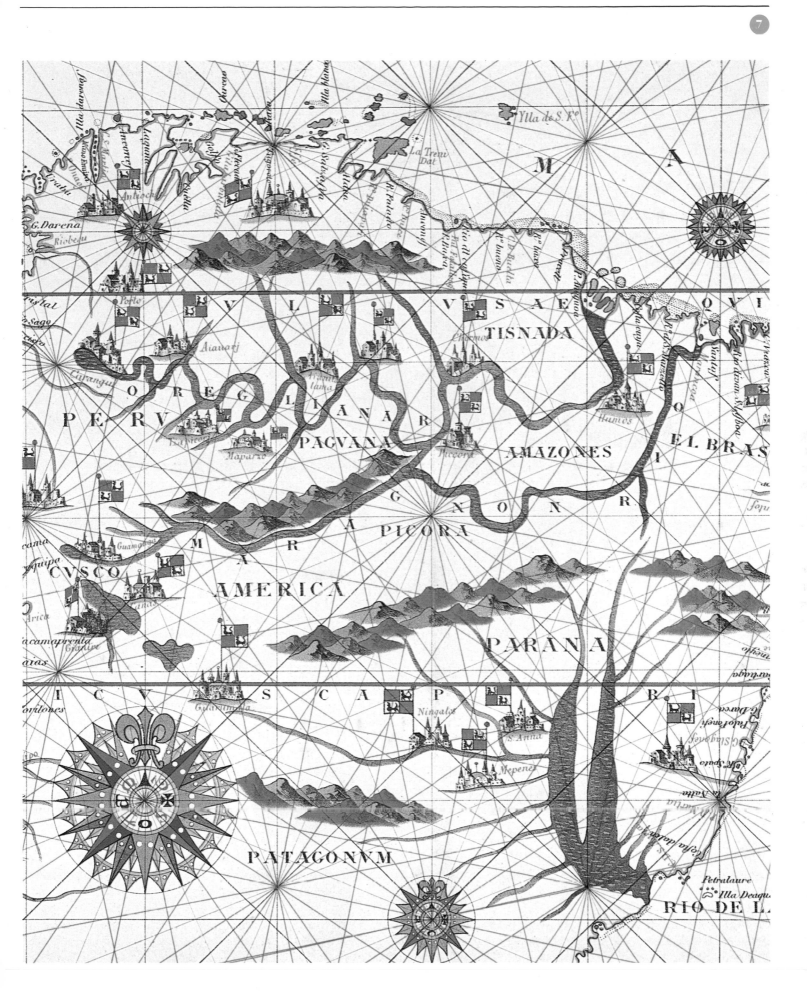

1

X Marks the Spot

The chances of tracing pirate hauls, or any other form of hidden wealth, except by accident, recede the further one goes back in history. If records exist at all, they have usually become distorted over the years, or embellished by repetition to the point where any factual basis has disappeared under layers of myth. So would-be seekers of pirate gold must turn to more recent events, where there is at least some possibility of sifting fact from fiction. Effectively, that denotes a period from the Middle Ages onwards.

Modern piracy is generally held to have had its beginnings in the 13th century. Most of the pirates of the age retained at least nominal fealty to their rulers — among them the French corsairs who operated from the Channel ports from Dunkirk to St Malo, and from Nantes and La Rochelle in the Bay of Biscay. They were privately financed by local merchants, and at first their victims were English trade ships. Later, they extended their depredations to vessels of any maritime power with which France was in dispute, and eventually they were granted official status as licensed privateers whose activities were approved by the French Minister of the Navy. (The system of privateering, in which individual captains were given free rein to harass enemy shipping and ports, lasted into the 19th century.)

In most cases, the corsairs handed over their booty to their backers, retaining only a small portion for themselves and their crews as a sort of fee for their work. But occasionally greed got the better of them, and they concealed part of the haul, intending to reclaim it later. There are several legends of corsair prizes hidden along the French Channel coast.

The rise of deep-sea piracy

On his first trip to the Americas, Columbus acquired gold nuggets from Hispaniola. When he displayed them at the court of King Ferdinand and Queen Isabella of Spain, he unleashed a bout of gold fever such as the world had never seen. The Portuguese had already discovered a new source of the precious metal at Elmina in the Gold Coast (now Ghana), and the Spaniards had no wish to be left behind. By the mid-1500s, the stage was set for full-blooded ransacking of the new territories. Gold, silver, jewels, and precious artifacts were being sent by the boatload back to Spain, offering prizes that no official enemy or independent pirate could resist. Since that time they have provided a constant thread in the annals of treasure hunting, exerting a lure as powerful now as it was two or three centuries ago. The newfound wealth of Spain and, to a lesser extent, Portugal attracted the envious eyes of many from the start. The corsairs of France were the first into the fray; in 1522, Jean d'Ango of Dieppe captured Spanish caravels carrying 45,000 gold pesos from Mexico, in a battle off the Azores. Soon men like François le Clerc, nicknamed 'Wooden Leg', and Jacques de Sores were raiding Spanish bases in the West Indies. De Sores held Havana for nearly three weeks in 1555, cramming his ships with gold and silver, slaughtering the inhabitants and burning the settlement to the ground.

Sir Francis Drake

Prominent among English seafarers of the same period was Francis Drake, who raided settlements up and down the Panama coast, including the port of Nombre de Dios, nicknamed 'the world's treasure-store', and captured more than 100 Spanish vessels. His most glittering prize was the treasure ship *Nuestra Señora de la Concepción* in the Pacific off Ecuador, carrying 13 chests of coins, 80 lb of gold bars, and 26 tons of silver. That exploit earned Drake a knighthood from Queen Elizabeth I in 1580 and made him one of the richest and most admired men in England. His exploits inspired generations of pirates on the Spanish Main, and provided early authenticated examples of two traditional ingredients of any quest for pirate treasure — secret charts and a buried cache.

The charts came from *Nuestra Señora de la Concepción* and showed the route used by Spanish galleons sailing laden with silks and spices from the Philippines to Mexico. They provided valuable clues for modern-day treasure seekers. The treasure cache was somewhere on the Caribbean side of the Isthmus of Panama, near the Royal Road along which the Spaniards brought gold and silver for trans-shipment across the Atlantic.

Barbary corsairs harry Spain

From the early 1500s, before their treasure fleets were menaced by their north European rivals, the Spaniards faced a maritime threat much nearer home. It came from the feared Barbary corsairs, Muslim pirates operating from bases on the North African coast and owing loose allegiance to the rulers of Turkey.

Hernán Cortés (1485-1547) led a force of 600 Spanish conquistadores in subjugating Mexico from 1519 onward — an invasion that laid the basis for Spain's power and wealth in the Americas, and for three centuries of treasure shipments from the New World to the Old. In the 16th-century painting above, the Spanish conquistadores are shown on horseback; they introduced the horse to America.

Far right:

Montezuma II (right) was ruler of the Aztec empire from 1502 to 1520. His gold-rich kingdom attracted the attentions of the Spanish then establishing themselves in the New World, and Montezuma was captured by Hernán Cortés (left) in 1519 and later killed by his own subjects.

The Spaniards were the corsair's main target, but they regarded all Christian nations with the same contemptuous hatred, plundering the French and the Venetians with almost equal fervor. In the 16th century, Algiers was the corsairs' headquarters; one of their number, Arouj, known as Barbarossa from his red beard, at one stage became ruler of the city by the simple expedient of murdering the Emir. His cruelty was such that the Spaniards and the Algerians joined forces against him. Barbarossa fled into the desert scattering treasure behind him to try to distract his pursuers, but they caught and killed him. Command of the corsairs went to this brother, Kheyr-ed-Din, who shared the family red hair and his brother's nickname, but was a much shrewder leader. He strengthened ties with Turkey, led corsair raids on Spanish vessels en route from the New World in the Atlantic, and drove the Spaniards out of North Africa.

European pirates in the Mediterranean

In the latter years of England's war against Spain in the 16th century, English ships had begun to appear in the Mediterranean, ostensibly to harry the Spaniards there, but they were not above raiding vessels of other nations if these offered rich pickings. Soon dozens of English seamen were cruising the Mediterranean, providing the truth of a comment by the contemporary French historian Joseph Scaliger: 'None make better pirates than the English.'

In 1604, England's peace treaty with Spain and James I's disapproval of privateering made these freebooters pirates in English law as well as in Spanish. They needed a local base, and found it in Tunis, where the Turkish ruler gave them refuge in return for the right to buy their plunder at very favorable prices.

Algiers, the old headquarters of the Barbary corsairs, was not so welcoming as Tunis to European renegades. In 1609, the acting English consul, Richard Allen, seized three Turkish vessels carrying cargo valued at 300,000 pieces-of-eight and fled with them to Spain. A year later, a Flemish freebooter called Simon Danser went one better, seizing 400,000 crowns and four ships in which he headed for

Marseilles, slaughtering some 150 Turks in the process.

By 1621, when the English navy blockaded Algiers, there were few Europeans left there. The same was true of Tunis. In their heyday, between 1592 and 1609, the Mediterranean corsairs had captured an average of 140 to 160 vessels a year.

Into the Atlantic

The peace of 1604, between England and Spain after nearly 20 years of constant warfare at sea, left England with a large, and now superfluous, reserve of battle-hardened sailors, most of whom were unfitted or disinclined to seek their livelihoods ashore. It was natural and inevitable that many should turn their experience to good account on their own behalf, as pirates. Once the decision was taken, there was little chance of going back, in the strict climate of James I's reign.

Some looked to the Mediterranean and the Barbary Coast for spoils and havens. But to many, the Atlantic offered more attractive opportunities. During the years of war, some licensed privateers who had strayed over the line into piracy, or gone 'on the account' in the slang of the day, were able to use English coves or harbors as bases, notably in Devon and Cornwall, remote from the authorities in London. But after 1604 that became extremely risky if not impossible, and the Atlantic pirates looked elsewhere. Two areas particularly commended themselves — Morocco and the west coast of Ireland. Thanks to Henry Mainwaring, an Oxford scholar who briefly turned pirate and then wrote a book on piracy, we have the earliest detailed picture of how the sea-raiders operated. More important for the treasure seeker, his work, called *Of the Beginnings, Practices and Suppression of Pirates*, lists in detail the pirates' main ports of call in the early 17th century — an excellent starting point for a search for relics.

In Morocco, the pirates made their headquarters at Mamora, near the Moorish pirate citadel of Sallee. But Mamora was not a satisfactory base for long. Both the Spaniards and the Dutch managed to blockade it — the Spaniards in 1611 sank ships across the harbor entrance, and in 1614 a Spanish fleet finally captured the town.

The rugged coast of Ireland, with its countless inlets and a population both remote

from the authorities in London and Dublin and contemptuous of them, was a far better bet. Most of the pirates made their headquarters around Roaringwater Bay, in the extreme southwest, with Leamcon as their main base. Pirate colonies also grew up on Long Island and Sherkin Island and, farther north, on Whiddy Island in Bantry Bay.

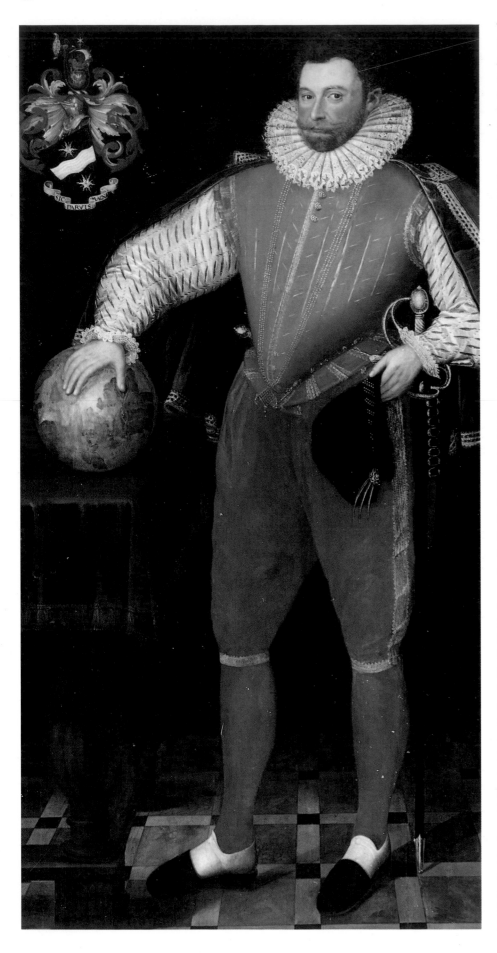

The golden age

In 1628, a Dutch fleet under the command of Admiral Pieter Hein succeeded in waylaying a convoy of Spanish treasure ships off the coast of Cuba, forcing them into Matanzas Bay, where they were wrecked on sandbanks. Reports of the number of Spanish vessels vary, but there could have been as many as 24. In any case, the Dutch had to refloat four of them to help carry the vast booty home, as all 28 Dutch ships were laden to the gunwales with treasure. Even so, they did not take all of it, and some is reputed still to lie on the bed of the bay. The exploit helped to inspire the growing bands of European corsairs, criminals and deserters flocking to the Spanish Main in search of their fortunes. They made their base on Tortuga, a small forested island now known as Tortue just off the north coast of Haiti. It eventually grew into an important haven for pirates, and even now has not yielded up all its secrets.

Renegades from the Low Countries soon joined the French, among them Alexander Exquemelin, whose book *De Americaensche Zee-Roovers* (Buccaneers of the Americas) is almost as useful to modern-day treasure seekers as Mainwaring's work of 60 years earlier, and Roche Brasiliano, who specialized in lightning assaults on Spanish settlements such as Campeche in Mexico. Together, they ushered in what has been called 'the golden age of piracy'.

English pirates, driven from their eastern Atlantic hunting grounds by improved naval patrols, also came to the Caribbean in growing numbers. Some found refuge at Tortuga and Le Petit Goave, off the west coast of Haiti. However, Port Royal in Jamaica was far more welcoming. From there, Henry Morgan sailed on his raids to Maracaibo in Venezuela — like Campeche, one of the pirates' favorite targets — and the stronghold of Panama City. Port Royal's role as a pirate base lasted until 1692, when an earthquake tipped half of the town into the sea. The submerged site is a favorite hunting ground for treasure seekers.

The pirates go east

Now that Port Royal was no longer available to them, the pirates began to look for more suitable havens. One group, led by the Englishman John Avery and the American Henry Tew, shifted its sphere of operations

to the Red Sea and the Indian Ocean, based on Madagascar, where St Mary's Island (Ile Ste Marie) gained almost as much notoriety as Port Royal had once enjoyed. It was to St Mary's Island that William Kidd sailed in 1698 after apparently turning from pirate-hunting to pirate. At the southern tip of Madagascar, at Ranter Bay, another collection of pirates installed themselves under a self-styled 'king', the Jamaican-born James Plantain.

Northeast of Madagascar, the islands of the Seychelles were another favorite pirate haven. In the 1720s, the notorious Frenchman Olivier Le Vasseur, nicknamed 'The Buzzard', based himself there to prey on shipping, and one of his prizes was a vessel carrying $140 million in treasure belonging to the Bishop of Goa, the Portuguese colony in India. Le Vasseur was eventually caught and hanged; as he went to the gallows he threw a paper to the crowd, bearing a cryptic message indicating where the Goan treasure was hidden.

Years later, it came into the hands of a former East African big-game hunter called Reginald Wilkins. He narrowed the location of the site down to Bel Ombre Bay on the island of Mahi, an area of underground caves and tunnels. Wilkins believed he was within six yards of the cache when he died in 1977. Since then, the site has been neglected and become overgrown. Recent surveys revealed a metal object the size of a dining table in the sand of

the bay. Plans to investigate it further were prepared, but no details of the outcome had been publicly announced by 1991.

Back to the Americas

For a while, Nassau in the Bahamas provided a refuge for pirates, at least for those who could bribe the governor. Avery was attempting to do just that when his ship, the *Fancy*, foundered on a reef outside the harbor, carrying at least some treasure to the value of $420,000. It has never been traced. Nassau had earlier been a base for the fearsome Edward Teach, known as 'Blackbeard', who terrorized merchantmen in the waters from Virginia to Florida between 1716 and 1718. It is said that he kept his treasure in a secret underground vault, where he also periodically walled up a succession of his wives.

By the early 1800s, the golden age of piracy was drawing to a close; almost its final flourish was provided by America's most notorious pirates, the brothers Jean and Pierre Lafitte. They operated from Barataria Bay on the coast of Louisiana, an inlet entered from a narrow channel between the islands of Grande Terre and Grande Ile, which the Lafittes fortified with cannon.

In 1814, the British navy tried in vain to enlist the Lafittes' support in the war against the United States. Eventually the Americans enlisted the pirates' help in defeating the

Above:

The great medieval trading organization known as the Hanseatic League, with its bases in all the main European ports around the Baltic and North Sea, was one of the earliest targets for organized piracy. A gang of seaborne raiders, who called themselves 'Friends of God and Enemies of the World', preyed on Hanseatic shipping. In 1402, one of the pirate leaders, Stertebeker (or Stoertebeck), and 70 of his accomplices were captured and executed at Hamburg. This 16th-century picture shows the pirates lined up for the executioner's sword.

Far left:

A hero to the English, a pirate to the Spanish, Sir Francis Drake (?1540-96) commanded a marauding fleet off Spanish America from 1585. He captured more than 100 Spanish vessels, including the treasure-laden Nuestra Señora de la Concepción, *and his exploits fired the imaginations of many during the golden age of piracy.*

British in the Battle of New Orleans. In return, they received a letter of thanks and free pardons — not nearly enough, in Jean Lafitte's view. He went back to piracy, operating from an island off the coast of Texas. That base was destroyed by the US navy in 1821, but Jean Lafitte escaped to re-emerge later under a false name in the guise of a respectable merchant, a role he successfully maintained until his death in 1854.

Tales are still told in the bayous of Louisiana of hidden caches made by the Lafitte brothers, although the evidence suggests that most of the treasure they accumulated was either disposed of or seized by the authorities. One thing is certain, however, in their lifetimes, old-style piracy virtually vanished.

A seeker's guide

For treasure-seekers looking for likely hiding places — the islands of the Caribbean and the American Atlantic seaboard, the west coast of Ireland, Madagascar, and the islands of the Indian Ocean, for example — several points are worth bearing in mind. First, both pirates and their victims generally played down the values of their hauls.

Second, there was little incentive for out-and-out rogues from the 17th century onwards to bury their treasure. Exceptions might arise if a haul was too great to be carried off in the available vessels, or if returning pirates got wind of an imminent raid on their base. Searches around such bases could yield a huge cache — but are more likely to reveal small (though valuable) quantities of items overlooked or lost.

The group with the biggest incentive to conceal treasure in remote places were privateers who went to the bad — a category that may embrace the likes of Kidd and Morgan. Even if the crews did not know the precise hiding place, they must have known the rough location, from where the ship put in and a few people went ashore. Back at base, and in their cups, some must have dropped heavy hints to anyone who would listen.

That is why tales of Morgan's treasure, spoken of by his crew though not by him, ring more true than those of Kidd, attested only by himself — and why a study of the privateers may ultimately be more rewarding than pursuit of the likes of Blackbeard.

The quest for Kidd's cache

When Captain William Kidd was hanged for piracy at London's Execution Dock on 23rd May 1701, he can hardly have foreseen the legacy he was leaving to future generations. For Kidd, more than any other person, has provided the basis for the stereotype pirate, possessor of the secret of a hidden treasure hoard. The stereotype has been embellished by a succession of writers of fiction who have drawn upon Kidd's exploits as source material — among them James Fenimore Cooper, Edgar Allan Poe and, above all, Robert Louis Stevenson in *Treasure Island.*

Stevenson's classic novel contains all the ingredients we have come to expect in a pirate yarn — a cryptic map, a mysterious island, buried gold, mayhem, murder, and the thrill of the quest. Some of these ingredients occurred in the lives of real pirates, but Kidd's history contains every one, in full measure.

Kidd's place both in romantic fiction and in the annals of treasure hunting was secured by a dramatic act on the eve of his execution. In a desperate attempt to save himself from the gallows, he wrote to the Speaker of England's House of Commons promising to reveal the whereabouts of some of his accumulated spoils in return for his life.

Said Kidd: 'In my proceedings in the Indies, I have lodged goods and Treasure to the value of £1000,000, which I desiere the Government may have the benefit of, in order thereto I shall desiere no manner of liberty, but to be kept prisoner on board such ship as may be appointed for that purpose and only give the necessary directions. And in case I faile therein, I shall desiere no favour but to be forthwith executed according to my sentence.'

Kidd's offer was ignored, and he duly went to his fate. Opinion at the time, shared by some experts now, was that the letter was a bluff. However, several powerful people in 18th-century England stood to benefit if Kidd, guilty or innocent, were silenced forever.

The Kidd legend flourished after his death. Then, more than 200 years later, in 1929, came the first solid piece of evidence that he may not have been bluffing after all. Hubert Palmer, a retired lawyer living in Eastbourne, England, bought a 17th-century oak desk bearing the inscription 'Captain William Kidd — Adventure Galley 1699'. Searching for secret compartments, Palmer accidentally broke one of the runners of the flap; inside he found a narrow brass tube with a parchment map wrapped around it. The map showed an island described as being in the China Sea, initialed 'WK' and dated 1699. Over the next five years, Palmer obsessively hunted down other relics of Kidd, finding three more maps in the process. All seemed to be of the same place, although the details varied. All seemed to be authentic, with handwriting that matched samples of Kidd's script, kept in the Public Records Office in London.

The discoveries sparked off a series of treasure hunts at various locations on America's eastern seaboard, in the Indian Ocean, and in the Sea of Japan, none of which, so far as is known, has yet yielded Kidd's hoard.

The making of a pirate

To anyone who knew Kidd before 1696, he would have seemed an unlikely candidate for infamy. Born in Scotland about 1645, he served in the English navy during the wars against the Dutch. Afterwards, he became a merchant, developing a successful trade with the Indies and eventually moving to New York, where he married a wealthy widow. Captain and Mrs Kidd moved in the upper echelons of New York society, and a record of 1689 describes him as a 'gentleman'.

But Kidd the merchant and society figure was still Kidd the sea captain. Between 1689 and 1695, he several times commanded a privateer, a private armed vessel licensed to harry the King's enemies — in this case, the French. At this time, it seems, Kidd had no thoughts of becoming a pirate. Indeed, his first privateer, the *Blessed William*, was stolen by his mutinous crew while it was undergoing repairs in Antigua. The men sailed off to raid shipping on their own account, but Kidd did not join them.

By 1695, the English government considered that pirates operating in the Atlantic and Indian oceans posed more of a threat to merchant shipping than the French did. But with England still at war with France, the navy could not be spared to rout the pirates out. So the newly appointed Governor of New York, the Earl of Bellomont, and several individual members of the government, including the First

Articles of Agreement,

Made the 10th Day of *October*, in the Year of our Lord 1695. Between the Right Honourable *RICHARD* Earl of *BELLOMONT* of the one part, and *Robert Levingston* Esq; AND

Captain William Kid,

Of the other part.

WHEREAS the said Capt. *William Kid* is desirous of obtaining a Commission as Captain of a Private Man of War in order to take Prizes from the King's Enemies, and otherways to annoy them; and whereas certain Persons did some time since depart from *New-England, Rode-Island, New-York*, and other parts in *America* and elsewhere, with an intention to become Pirates, and to commit Spoils and Depredations, against the Laws of Nations, in the *Red-Sea* or elsewhere, and to return with such Goods and Riches as they should get, to certain places by them agreed upon; of which said Persons and Places, the said Capt. *Kid* hath notice, and is desirous to fight with and subdue the said Pirates, as also other Pirates with whom the said Capt. *Kid* shall meet at Sea, in case he be impowered so to do; and whereas it is agreed between the said Parties, That for the purpose aforesaid a good and sufficient Ship, to the liking of the said Capt. *Kid*, shall be forthwith bought, whereof the said Capt. *Kid* is to have the Command. Now these Presents do witness, and it is agreed between the said Parties,

I. That the Earl of *Bellomont* doth covenant and agree, at his proper Charge, to procure from the King's Majesty, or from the Lords Commissioners of the Admiralty (as the Case shall require) one or more Commissions, impowering him the said Capt. *Kid* to act against the King's Enemies, and to take Prizes from them, as a private Man of War in the usual manner; and also to fight with, conquer and subdue Pirates, and to take them and their Goods; with other large and beneficial Powers and Clauses in such Commissions as may be most proper and effectual in such Cases.

II. The said Earl of *Bellomont* doth covenant and agree, That within three Months after the said Capt. *Kid's* departure from *England*, for the purposes in these Presents mentioned, he will procure, at his proper charge, a Grant from the King, to be made to some indifferent and trusty Person, of all such Merchandizes, Goods, Treasure and other things as shall be taken from the said Pirates, or any other Pirate whatsoever, by the said Capt. *Kid*, or by the said Ship, or any other Ship or Ships under his Command.

III. The said Earl doth agree to pay four Fifth parts, the whole in Five parts to be divided, of all Moneys which shall be laid out for the buying such good and sufficient Ship for the purposes aforesaid, together with Rigging and other Apparel and Furniture thereof, and providing the same with competent victualling the said Ship, to be approved of by the said Parties; and the said other one Fifth part of the said Charges of the said Ship to be paid for by the said *Robert Levingston* and *William Kid*.

IV. The said Earl doth agree, That in order to the speedy buying the said Ship, in part of the said four parts of Five of the said Charges, he will pay down the sum of sixteen hundred Pounds, by way of Advance, on or before the sixth day of *November* next ensuing.

V. The said *Robert Levingston* and *William Kid* do jointly and severally covenant and agree, That on and before the sixth day of *November*, when the said Earl of *Bellomont* is to pay the said Sum of sixteen hundred pounds as aforesaid, they will advance and pay down four hundred pounds in part of the Share and Proportion which they are to have in the said Ship.

Far left:

Kidd went to the gallows at London's notorious Execution Dock in May 1701, despite his eve-of-hanging promise to reveal the whereabouts of booty he claimed to have concealed. Kidd's body, like that of many a pirate before him, was afterwards displayed in chains on a gibbet as a visible reminder of the price of crime. This illustration is from The Pirate's Own Book *(1837), which inspired many a pirate yarn.*

Above:

The fateful agreement of 1695 with the Earl of Bellomont eventually brought Kidd to the gallows. In it, Bellomont undertakes to obtain for Kidd a commission as a privateer, and to underwrite the captain's expenses in return for a share of the spoils. What Kidd did not know is that Bellomont was acting as front man for a syndicate of highly-placed public figures, including King William III of England.

Lord of the Admiralty and the Chancellor, agreed on the plan that was eventually to bring Kidd to Execution Dock.

They decided to finance an unofficial expedition against the pirates, in return for secret shares in the booty, and Kidd was appointed to lead it. The veteran captain knew that Bellomont, who was to get a 60 percent share, was the main promoter. He did not know that his other backers were even more powerful figures, including the king himself,

William III, who was to get 10 percent.

For more than a year, Kidd's ship, the *Adventure Galley*, sailed the Atlantic and Indian Oceans without taking a significant prize. Wracked by disease and with supplies running low, the crew became mutinous, knowing that their only pay was to be a share of the booty. Matters came to a head when Kidd declined to attack a Dutch East Indiaman — which he was forbidden to do under his letter of commission, but which the crew by now expected. In the

Right:
This pirate-style map of the Caribbean shows the hunting grounds of the buccaneers of the Spanish Main. By conscious or unconscious irony, the two ships depicted are placed near the sites of famous treasure wrecks.

brooding atmosphere, Kidd killed his gunner, whom he suspected of fomenting mutiny, with a blow from an iron-bound bucket.

A fateful decision

The incident seems to have made up Kidd's mind, and from then on he launched attacks on ships and settlements of many nations. His greatest prize was the *Quedah Merchant*, an Armenian vessel commanded by an Englishman and carrying French safe-conduct passes. With

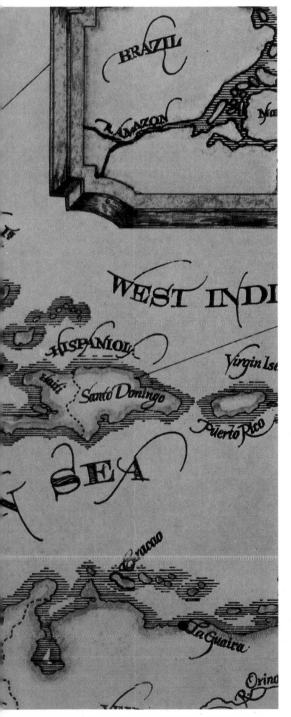

the *Quedah Merchant* and another Armenian ship, the *Maiden*, in tow, Kidd sailed to St Mary's Island, near Madagascar, a nest of the very pirates he was supposed to eradicate. There, he was apparently made welcome; the spoils were divided, and Kidd sailed for New York in the *Quedah Merchant*, having abandoned the *Adventure Galley* as unseaworthy. Meanwhile, the Admiralty in London had received reports of Kidd's attack on a fellow English captain, albeit of a foreign ship. Kidd was declared a pirate, a fact he learned in the West Indies on the voyage home. He changed vessels again, to the sloop *Antonio*, and made several calls along the American coast before finally putting ashore at Boston. Kidd was apparently expecting protection from Bellomont, but the governor promptly had him arrested and shipped in irons back to England, where he languished for more than a year in London's Newgate prison before coming to trial.

By that time Bellomont was dead, and both the first Lord of the Admiralty and the Chancellor had been impeached for their part in the expedition. The whole affair had become a scandal threatening the government and even the monarchy. Public opinion had already condemned Kidd, and none of his previous supporters was prepared to risk his position by intervening. His death sentence was almost a foregone conclusion.

Below:
Friends in high places did not dare to intervene to save Captain William Kidd when he was arraigned for piracy before the House of Commons in London. He was unable to produce vital evidence on his own behalf and was duly sentenced to death, leaving behind him one of the most enduring stories of hidden pirate gold.

Where is Treasure Island?

Above:
A 19th-century print sold by
Pollock's Toy Theatre shop in
London purports to show William
Kidd in action, but it is a very
romanticized portrait. The shop
was a favorite browsing spot
for Robert Louis Stevenson
(1850-94), whose famous novel
Treasure Island *drew on Kidd's*
real-life career.

Top right:
Two versions of the treasure map
found in the early 20th century
and attributed to Kidd. The lower,
more detailed version clearly
places the island in the China Sea.
But letters in the cross-hatching
on the left of the island spell out
the word 'oak' — perhaps a
reference to Oak Island off the
coast of Nova Scotia. The writing
around the border is assumed to
contain instructions on how to
locate the treasure, while the
cryptic reference to '20 turtles'
may be a clue that the map is in
fact upside down.

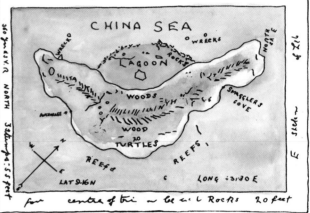

The legend of Captain Kidd's 'treasure island' rapidly gained impetus after his death, and the value of the treasure multiplied into millions, although there is no firm evidence that Kidd acquired much more than the gold, silver, jewelry and silks from the *Quedah Merchant* and the *Maiden* during his brief spell of piracy. Some of that loot was shared out among the crew who remained in Madagascar when Kidd put in there in 1698, and more was given to seamen who left the sloop *Antonio* at Lewes in Delaware Bay before Kidd arrived in Boston in July 1699. We also know that, prior to his arrival in Boston, Kidd moored at Gardiner's Island, off Long Island, and deposited bales and chests, including at least one containing gold. However, those goods were quickly traced and collected by Lord Bellomont.

Sceptics argue that the original tales of Kidd's treasure grew up around his activities on Gardiner's Island, and were fueled by his eve-of-execution letter. The letter remains the only authenticated primary evidence that the treasure exists at all. The maps found by Palmer all came from genuine sea chests of Kidd's era, bearing Kidd's name. And the writing on them does appear to match that of Kidd. But, say the sceptics, for one man to discover no fewer than four pirate maps, after more than 200 years stretches coincidence a very long way.

The most explicit of the charts appeared in 1934, inside a chest inscribed 'William and Sarah Kidd, their Chest'. It gives the latitude and longitude of the island, as well as coded instructions about where the treasure is hidden. But in those days, latitude was not universally calculated from the Greenwich meridian, so the bearings on the chart are of little use. In addition, the code is obscure. Another complicating factor is that the island is clearly stated to be in the China Sea. So far as is known, Kidd did not visit that area during his voyage of 1696-99.

A Japanese discovery

According to one theory, the island may be Yokoate, which is part of a group stretching from southern Japan toward Taiwan. In 1952, some Japanese fishermen took shelter in an bay there. Exploring ashore, they found carvings of a horned animal on a rock face. The discovery eventually came to the attention of the Japanese scholar Nagashima, who remembered that Kidd had sometimes used a stylized drawing of a young goat as his mark — a pun on his surname.

Nagashima investigated the spot, where he is rumored to have found the entrance to a cave almost entirely covered by undergrowth. Inside, it is said, a heap of old iron boxes contained some $50 million in gold and silver coins, which Nagashima had shipped back to Tokyo in conditions of great secrecy. Subsequently, Japanese newspapers reported that Nagashima had vanished, allegedly taking the treasure with him, and that he was being sought by the police.

Whether or not Nagashima did find Kidd's treasure, there are plenty of people who argue that the China Sea reference on the charts is correct. They contend that the maps, or perhaps a lost original from which they were copied, do not denote a cache actually made by Kidd, but were acquired by him at some stage during his career as a privateer. The theory conveniently explains one mystery — why a prosperous merchant should accept a risky commission to do battle with pirates. Kidd's aim all along, it is said, was to use the opportunity of the *Adventure Galley* voyage to try to find the China Sea island for himself, making and concealing various copies of the chart in case one was lost or stolen.

Those who support this view also say that it explains why Kidd, in his last letter, was not more specific about the location of the treasure — because he did not know it precisely himself. On the other hand, as he was bargaining for his life and was by no means a fool, why should he have given full information to his captors until he had secured a promise of mercy?

Other islands

Another school of thought maintains that the China Sea location is merely a blind, intended to put anyone stumbling on the map accidentally off the scent, and that Kidd really buried the treasure much nearer home. The Caribbean is a possible site, as it was there that Kidd abandoned the *Quedah Merchant* in favor of the *Antonio*. Certainly, in his subsequent dealings with Bellomont, Kidd made much of the treasure that he said he had left on the *Quedah Merchant*. This claim does not ring true because by then the vessel had been reduced to a hulk, and would almost certainly have been looted. If, however, Kidd had concealed the cargo somewhere on the islands, and was using the ship's name as a sort of

shorthand for Bellomont, the story would make more sense. But no real evidence has been found to support it.

The most intriguing theory, though, places Kidd's island much farther north, off the coast of Nova Scotia. It is called Oak Island, and it has been under investigation by treasure-seekers since 1804, without yet yielding all its mysteries.

Above:

Another romanticized view of Kidd, this time supervising the burial of treasure on Gardiner's Island, off the coast of New York. Kidd did deposit booty there some time in 1699, but so far as is known all of it was recovered by the authorities soon afterwards.

The puzzle of Panama

Below:

In this 17th-century map of the Isthmus of Panama, north is at the bottom and the Pacific Ocean appears at the top. Morgan's raiders landed on the Caribbean coast and made their way south toward Panama City (bottom) along the Chagres, the river that meanders across the center of the map. Their perilous journey took them nine days. Their aim was to surprise the Spanish defenders of Panama City, who were not accustomed to attacks from land. But the Spanish learned in advance they were coming, and incompetence, rather than surprise, caused the city to fall.

In the 17th century, Panama City was the richest settlement in the whole of the New World, a storehouse of gold and silver wrested from the Incas by their Spanish conquerors. Its vast wealth had drawn the greedy eyes of privateers and pirates from Drake's time onwards, but the city was heavily defended against seaward attack from the Pacific, and seemingly protected by thick jungle against an onslaught by land. However, the city's solid defenses proved no match for one of the most notorious raiders of the Spanish Main, Captain Henry Morgan.

In 1670, Morgan assembled a fleet of 36 ships and nearly 2,000 men for the biggest-ever raid on Spanish territories. Once out from Port Royal, the force agreed that Panama City should be the target. The fleet anchored off the mouth of the Chagres River, on the Caribbean side of the Isthmus of Panama, and Morgan and 1,400 men began the nine-day journey by sea and land to the Pacific coast.

News of their impending arrival had reached the Spaniards in Panama, and cavalry and infantry were mobilized to defend the city. Unfortunately for the Spanish, the terrain on which they chose to fight was unsuitable for cavalry, and a herd of cattle, which the defenders had intended to drive into Morgan's battle line, stampeded and threw the infantry into disarray. The Spaniards fled, putting the city itself to the torch.

Once the flames had died down, Morgan and his men rampaged through the city in search of treasure. Eventually the raiders left, taking with them 175 mules laden with plate, gold and silver coins, and jewelry, and sowing the seeds of a mystery that continues to intrigue treasure-hunters to this day.

The lost fortune

The mule train, although carrying a fortune, did not represent anything like the spoils that might have been expected from Panama City.

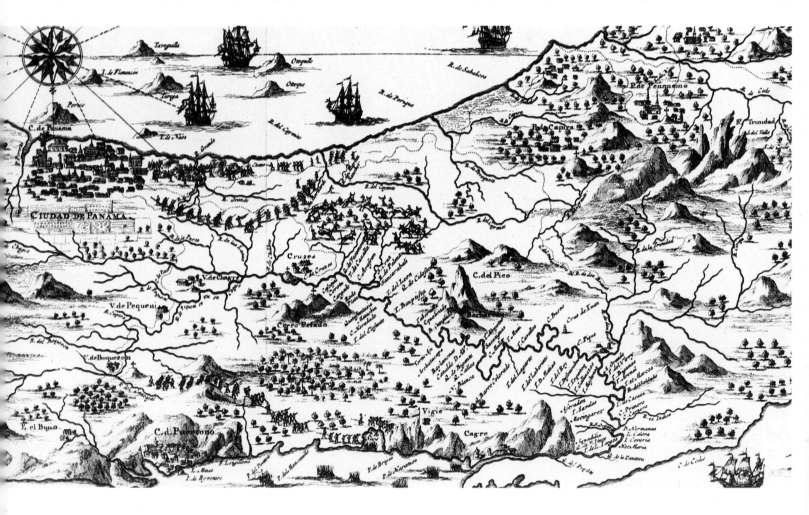

Morgan's raid had been by land, so the harbor had not been blockaded, and at least one Spanish treasure ship, and possibly others, made good its escape.

A large portion of the valuable loot which had been brought out by mules appeared to have vanished when the survivors came to share it out back at their ships. They received just £10 a head which, even when multiplied a hundredfold to equal modern values, was a paltry sum after all their privations. Morgan himself slipped away on his ship, having ordered cannon from the captured fort of San Lorenzo to be installed on board. The clear implication was that he had seized the best part of the booty for his ends.

The English government, which stood to gain a share of the treasure as Morgan was operating as a privateer, clearly believed it had been swindled. On his return to Jamaica, Morgan was arrested and shipped back to England to face charges of piracy. Unlike the luckless William Kidd, however, Morgan was a popular hero. His trial never took place, and he eventually returned to the Caribbean as Lieutenant-Governor of Jamaica, where he became the scourge of English and Spanish pirates alike before dying of drink and dissipation at the age of 53.

During his lifetime, Morgan made no reference to treasure he had hidden, although his former shipmates did. There are many who believe that the hoard remains to be found somewhere in the Caribbean between Panama and Jamaica.

Above left:
Henry Morgan (?1635-88)
captured the seemingly
impregnable Spanish base of
Panama City in 1670 on behalf
of the British. He stripped it of its
lavish treasures, but when the
spoils came to be shared out there
was little enough for his crew. For
three centuries people have
speculated about what happened
to the rest of Morgan's booty.
Some believe it is buried near
Panama, others that it is hidden
on one of the islands that dot
the Caribbean.

Above:
The name of Morgan cast as much
fear into the Spanish as that of
Drake had done a century earlier.
In this 18th-century engraving,
Morgan (left foreground) is
depicted loading the sack of Port
au-Prince (Puerto del Principe),
a Spanish settlement in Cuba.

The Coco Island hoards

As early as 1683 one area of what is now Costa Rican territory began to earn a reputation as a potential source of incalculable wealth, a reputation it still possesses today. The area is the Ile del Coco, an island 300 miles southwest of the Costa Rican mainland, in the Pacific. There, at least three, and possibly several more, pirate hoards are known to have been concealed.

Among the first to take advantage of this knowledge was the Englishman Captain Edward Davis, one of a group of notorious buccaneers whose other members included John Coxon, Bartholomew Sharp and William Dampier. The last-named later gained respectability as a navigator and writer, sailing around the world three times. Some of these high-spirited adventurers were as ignorant and careless as they were brave.

Davis was shrewder than most of his colleagues. In his ship *Bachelor's Delight* he emerged periodically from Coco to prey on Spanish vessels and coastal towns such as Guayaquil in Ecuador. The biggest prize of all, the Lima treasure fleet, eluded him, because a French force with which he allied himself stood off while Davis unsuccessfully took on the Spaniards. However, he amassed enough booty to retire temporarily to Florida during King James II's amnesty for pirates, before taking up piracy again and disappearing mysteriously about 1702.

Bonito's bonanza

The remote island also provided a suitable hideaway for another pirate, more than 100 years after Davis' presumed death, the Portuguese Benito Bonito. In 1819, Bonito plundered a cargo of gold from the Mexican port of Acapulco and, returning to Coco, hid it in Wafer Bay. Two years later, the pirate was killed in an engagement with a British man-o'-war in the West Indies, so he could not reclaim his treasure.

Unlike Davis, however, Bonito left clues to the whereabouts of the cache. In 1880, the grandson of one of the men who had sailed with Bonito revealed a treasure map to a German sailor called Gissler. It showed an island which the old pirate had called 'Las

Palmas'. Gissler copied the map and, eight years later in Hawaii, came across another map. By comparing them, he concluded that the island in question was Coco. He eventually settled on Coco and spent 20 years there searching for the treasure. During that time he went through considerable hardship, including a raid by two English cruisers bent on seizing any booty for themselves. The English found nothing, and Gissler was not much luckier. All he had to show for two decades of effort was one Spanish doubloon dated 1788. He died penniless in New York in 1930.

By a supreme irony, Bonito's hoard was located just two years after Gissler's death by treasure seekers using the newly invented metal detector. The gold was found more or less where the maps showed it would be — proof that at least some pirate charts are accurate.

Looking the Thompson's haul

The location of the third, and potentially the most valuable, of the Coco treasures was also plotted on a map, drawn on his deathbed by the Scotsman William Thompson, the man who originally hid it. This cache — part of the vast wealth amassed by the Spanish civil and religious authorities during nearly three centuries' occupation of Peru — is the biggest attraction on Coco for treasure-seekers.

Left:
At least two hoards are thought to be buried on Ile del Coco (Coco Island), probably somewhere at the northern tip in the area around Wafer Bay and Chatham Bay. It was there that, in 1932, treasure seekers using a metal detector found gold concealed in the 19th century by the buccaneer Benito Bonito. The island's biggest prize, priceless treasure removed from Lima in Peru in 1823, has yet to yield itself up.

Far left:
Dense shrubs cover most of the Ile del Coco in the Pacific, a pirates' hideaway from the 17th to the 19th century.

COCOS ISLAND
(densely covered with trees and bushes)

NORTH PACIFIC OCEAN
COCOS ISLAND

Left:
A fanfare of publicity accompanied the British expedition to the Ile del Coco in 1932. This map appeared in a feature in The Illustrated London News *of the time. Other forays to the island have been conducted in far greater secrecy.*

Right:
Since the 1870s, the Ile del Coco
has been the destination of dozens
of treasure-hunting expeditions.
This British team visited the
island aboard SS Vigilant *in 1932.*

Our Lady of Lima

In 1823, the revolutionary armies of Simón Bolívar were driving the Spaniards from the South American empire they had built up over the previous three centuries. The liberator's forces were drawing near to Lima, capital of the viceroyalty of Peru and one of the wealthiest cities on the continent, throwing civil and church authorities into panic.

William Thompson's brig, the *Mary Dear*, lay at anchor in the port of Lima after a trade voyage, and the Spaniards, desperate to save their fortunes, quickly struck a deal with the captain. The *Mary Dear* was to take aboard a quantity of treasure, under Spanish guard, to prevent its falling into Bolívar's hands. If the city held out successfully against the revolutionaries, Thompson was to return with his cargo in a few weeks. If Lima capitulated, Thompson was to set a course for Panama City, then still a Spanish bastion, and offload the treasure there.

The precious items were transferred to the brig, and they represented a fortune, including a lifesize statue of the Madonna, crafted in solid gold. The *Mary Dear* swiftly slipped anchor.... But from the start, Thompson appears to have had no intention of observing his side of the bargain. Once at sea, he quickly disposed of the Spanish guards and headed for the Ile del Coco. Ashore, the bulk of the treasure was concealed in a cave and the rest shared out among Thompson's crew.

The Spaniards were not as trusting as they seemed, and Thompson was already under suspicion. The *Mary Dear* was captured by the frigate *Espiègle* and all hands, except for Thompson and the first mate, were put to death for theft and piracy. They were spared to guide the Spaniards to the main cache.

Back on Coco, the two men managed to elude their captors and hide while a fruitless search for the treasure was carried out. After a week, the Spaniards gave up and set sail, leaving Thompson and the mate marooned with their spoils. Another week went by before a whaler put into the island. The two buccaneers revealed themselves, though not the existence of the treasure, and were carried to safety.

The tell-tale map

The mate died, perhaps as the result of his ordeal, leaving Thompson the only man alive who knew the precise whereabouts of the Lima treasure. But try as he would, the Scotsman could not raise the money to return and claim it. In his later years, Thompson befriended a wandering seaman called John Keating, and it was to Keating that Thompson, on his deathbed, gave the treasure map.

Keating was luckier than Thompson had been. He soon found a financial backer to accompany him to Coco, and between them they located the cave, removing what they could carry in their pockets. Unfortunately, Keating's crew realized what was afoot and threatened to kill him unless he revealed the site of the cave. But Keating, like Thompson

before him, escaped and hid. The crew searched for the treasure in vain, then left. Keating was picked up by a passing ship several months later.

In 1875, a seaman called Bob Flower slipped through the undergrowth into a pit while exploring the island. Fearing for his life, he managed to scramble out quickly, but not before noticing some gold coins. When Flower tried to retrace the spot, he could not find it. Subsequent expeditions retrieved some items — a gold Madonna 2 ft high from the Bay of Hope, and 133 gold and silver coins from the same area.

Clues to the cache

One of the problems facing prospectors is knowing exactly what kind of site they are looking for. The cave features in the earliest records, but Keating also mentioned a stone with a letter K carved on it, and an arrow pointing to a hollow tree. The stone and tree — with a cable and hook attached to it — were traced around the turn of the century, but no sign of the treasure was found.

The mysterious money pit

Little Oak Island lies four miles off the coast of Nova Scotia, sheltered from the open ocean by other islands to seaward. At its eastern end, a natural shaft or blowhole apparently once led downward to a large cavern some 200 feet below the surface. The shaft has been blocked by a series of platforms and partially flooded through side tunnels to create a virtually inaccessible 'money pit' that, according to local legend, contains a massive store of treasure.

Almost certainly, the island was used as a haven by pirates in the 17th and 18th centuries, but there are flaws in the tales linking Kidd to Oak. It is just possible that the *Antonio* could have reached the island in its wanderings along the Atlantic coast before Kidd came ashore at Boston, but it is certain that he would not have had time then to prepare the complex money pit. Other possibilities remain. The pit may have already been in existence, simply waiting for Kidd to install his treasure and seal it; but that is unlikely, again because of time. The pit may have been prepared on some other occasion, by Kidd or someone else. Or Kidd may indeed have visited Oak in 1699, but hidden his treasure somewhere else entirely.

until 1795 that the money pit was discovered. A 16-year-old boy exploring the island noticed a circular depression in the ground and, with two friends, began to dig. The boys uncovered one platform of stone and two of logs before giving up. Nine years later, having found financial backers, the three returned and dug down to a depth of 98 feet before seawater flooded in.

Digging continues

In the 1840s, a syndicate was formed to excavate the pit by digging a new shaft parallel to the original. These efforts were equally unsuccessful, and the second shaft also flooded. For two years from 1909, Captain Harry L. Boudouin of New York tried his hand at excavation. His team was eventually forced to give up, and he declared in disgust, 'There was never a pirate or any other treasure in the money pit on Oak Island.' But his disappointment did not deter others, and a series of further expeditions visited the site.

By 1967, the depredations of the treasure-hunters had so churned up the eastern end of the island that all surface clues had disappeared in a sea of mud. However, one possibly significant piece of evidence was discovered — a stone dated 1704.

In 1970, a salvage company, Triton, launched the biggest onslaught on the money pit to date. Using modern equipment, the excavators plumbed the pit to a depth of 212 feet, some 40 feet lower than anyone had previously reached, and revealed the existence of the cave at the base of the shaft. Underwater cameras showed old logs piled on the cave floor and, it was said, three chests and a human hand apparently chopped off at the wrist.

First among the unanswered question is who built the pit, and when? The earliest evidence of activity is the dated stone, which seems to rule out a link with Kidd, because he had been dead for three years by 1704. But the pit may have been dug much later, in 1763, when the citizens of Chester noticed the strange lights. Yet the intriguing possibility that Kidd visited the island and hid treasure there, either before or after his last disastrous voyage, still exists.

The making of the pit

Whoever constructed the money pit was an engineer of great ability. The system of tunnels and platforms is arranged in such a way that anyone trying to reach the lowest platform, on which the treasure is presumed to rest, cannot do so without flooding the shaft entirely with seawater unless the tunnels, deep in the ground, can be dammed first.

The earliest records of possible pirate activity on Oak Island date from 1763, when residents in the settlement of Chester, across the bay, noticed 'strange lights and fires'. However, no one investigated, and it was not

Next page:
In this view of Little Oak Island, Nova Scotia, from the south, its shape can clearly be seen to resemble that on the treasure maps attributed to William Kidd. The existence of the money pit on Oak Island was already known when the maps began to appear earlier this century.

2

Abandon Ship

T he quest for pirate gold is one of the most romantic aspects of treasure hunting, but such gold is an elusive commodity. Almost as romantic, and far less elusive, are the wrecks littering the world's shipping lanes and coastal waters. For centuries, the approximate locations of major shipwrecks have been recorded — in particular if the vessels involved were carrying precious cargoes, or were symbols of national pride such as great warships or ocean liners.

The Nanking Cargo

In April 1986, Amsterdam was the venue for one of the biggest auctions of rediscovered treasure in history. It was not, however, a hoard of precious metals or cache of stolen jewels that brought collectors from all over the world to Holland, but 100,000 pieces of antique Chinese porcelain. After over 200 years at the bottom of the China Sea, the Nanking Cargo, as it had become known, had finally reached its destination.

Carefully packed into crates of tea, the porcelain had been the main cargo of a Dutch East Indiaman. The merchant ship, which remains unidentified, was on its homeward voyage from Canton to Europe some time in the 1750s. Unfortunately disaster struck and the ship went to the bottom, though by some miracle not violently enough to disturb its fragile cargo. Sealed like a time capsule beneath the waters for 200 years, the contents of the ship's hold remained intact and in mint condition, transforming the porcelain from simple articles of 18th-century commerce to treasure worth discovering.

It was rediscovered in the 1980s by British salvage expert Captain Michael Hatcher, a specialist on wrecks in the waters of the Far East. Hatcher was no stranger to delicate salvage operations, having discovered by accident in 1983 the wreck of a 17th-century Asian trading junk. The recovery of the cargo of this vessel revealed an astonishing 23,000 pieces of antique Chinese porcelain from the Ming period, in perfect condition.

The financial rewards for the salvage of such a treasure were brought home to Hatcher when the cargo (which has since become known as the Hatcher collection) was sold at auction for over $2 million!

Inspired by this success, and aided by Swiss-born surveyor Max de Rham, Hatcher began the search for other wrecks which culminated in the successful location and recovery of the Nanking Cargo in 1985.

The treasure itself is remarkable not only for the fact that it has been recovered in such pristine condition, but that so much of it has survived. The quantities are huge and display a dazzling variety. There are, for example, more than 40,000 tea bowls and saucers and enough tableware to assemble complete dinner services of more than 370 pieces with settings for 140 guests.

Attractive porcelain is all very well, of course, but included in the finds is a group of objects to whet the appetites of those who like their sunken treasure to have more of a metallic gleam Hatcher and his team also discovered gold.

In a small area just outside the hull of the wreck, divers discovered 125 gold ingots of two extremely rare Chinese types: the first, a series of cup-shaped ingots known as 'Nanking

Far left:
Part of the Nanking Cargo being raised from the seabed.

Below:
The Nanking Cargo was auctioned by Christie's Amsterdam between 28th April and 2nd May 1986. This picture shows part of a dinner service still intact inside the original crates in the ship's hold. The name of the ship was never discovered.

Shoes'; the second, a group of small rectangular ingots, about four inches long. Since no 18th-century Chinese gold of these types is known in the West, this particular find is worth as much perhaps for its historical value as for its value as bullion.

The earliest wrecks

In 1984, underwater archaeologists working off the Mediterranean coast of Turkey released details of an amazing find — the well-preserved wreck of a merchant ship that had plied the seas some 3,400 years ago, while Tutankhamun ruled Egypt and before the Ancient Greeks had fought the Trojan War. The nationality of the vessel is not known, but its cargo of Bronze Age goods showed that it had voyaged between Greece, Cyprus, and the lands of the early Phoenicians. To date, it is the earliest shipwreck found.

The meticulously excavated ship stirred the imagination of archaeologists, if not that of the general public. Its load of pottery and wine jars, although of considerable archaeological

importance, could not match the more glamorous treasures dredged up from later wrecks such as those of Spanish plate galleons or England's *Mary Rose*. Even so, it demonstrated two highly significant things: seawater, seabed silt, and marine accretions such as barnacles and weeds are remarkable preservatives of many ancient materials and artifacts; and underwater currents do not move items on the seabed nearly as much as had once been believed.

Those early wrecks that have been thoroughly excavated, such as the one off Turkey, have not been found to contain treasure in the conventional sense of the word. In most cases, their contents have consisted of pottery, wine jars, bronze goods, and marble in various stages of working—all of great interest to historians and archaeologists, but of little intrinsic value.

Precious items are generally lacking, too, in wrecks dating from the fall of Rome to the 15th century — for example, the five 11th-century ships raised at Riskilde in Denmark, the Venetian galley of about 1439 discovered in Italy's Lake Garda, and the 12th-century boat which was one of an incredible 156 vessels found when part of the Zuider Zee in Holland was drained in the 1950s. Possible exceptions are two Viking longships that went down somewhere off the Shetland Islands while returning to Norway after a series of raids in 1151. They are said to have been laden with gold and silver, but have never been found. However, it is only when we reach the 16th century, the beginnings of the great age of European exploration and conquest, that the true quest for marine treasure gets under way.

Wrecks of the Spanish Main

The golden era of piracy was born with Columbus' voyages to the New World, and the same might also be said of shipwrecks. For the richly laden vessels that drew the attention of the sea raiders were susceptible to other perils of the deep — currents, storms, rocks, reefs, and shallows. Nowhere was this more true than in the Caribbean and adjoining waters of the Atlantic, the region loosely known as the Spanish Main.

The first great wreck of a Spanish treasure fleet in the Caribbean consisted of 32 caravels, including the flagship *El Dorado*, that set sail from Hispaniola in July 1502 despite warnings

from Christopher Columbus himself of an impending hurricane. Aboard the *El Dorado* were Admiral Antonio de Torres, Governor Bobadilla of Hispaniola, an estimated $2 million in gold and silver, and a solid gold table said to have weighed 3,000 lb — Bobadilla's gift to the King and Queen of Spain. Columbus, who had just returned from Spain, watched helplessly as the vessels put to sea. Three days out, in the Mona Passage between the Dominican Republic and Puerto Rico, the hurricane struck, destroying the *El Dorado* and 25 other ships. The wrecks of some were later found on the reefs and beaches of the passage, but 17 have never been traced, among them the *El Dorado* with its precious table.

Bad weather struck a Spanish plate fleet in

Above:
Amphorae (wine jars) are among the artifacts most frequently retrieved from Ancient Greek and Roman wrecks in the Mediterranean. The area, like the Caribbean, is a favorite hunting ground for underwater explorers because of relatively high temperatures and good visibility, at least close to the coast.

Right and far right:
There are many old wrecks off the coast of Bermuda, providing great opportunities for underwater archaeology. These pictures show a cannon being found on the seabed and a diver investigating a wreck with the aid of a powerful hand-held torch.

1553 off Padre Island in what is now Texas. Out of 20 vessels, only three survived, and those shipwrecked sailors not drowned were slaughtered by hostile Indians ashore, whose presence is thought to have deterred contemporary efforts at salvage.

The Padre Island disaster was, in terms of ships and cargoes lost, one of the three biggest to hit a Spanish plate fleet. The other two occurred in 1715 and 1733, both off the Florida Keys. The tracing and salvage of vessels from the 1715 fleet is one of the most inspiring examples of amateur but responsible treasure hunting, yielding large quantities of valuable artifacts. To date, finds from the 1733 fleet have been relatively disappointing, probably because it was wrecked in very shallow water. The presumed remains of the flagship, the *Rui*,

were located in 1949, but earlier divers had not left much — some gold and silver coins, weapons, jewelry, and a silver statue of a dancer.

Losses increase

By the early part of the 17th century, sea traffic between the New World and Spain and, to a much lesser extent, Portugal, was at its height and so were the numerical losses of ships. In 1605, four galleons went down on the Serranilla Bank, midway between Central America and Jamaica. The Spaniards spent 60 years trying to find them and raise their cargoes, without success. In 1622, at least 15 vessels foundered along the Florida Keys from the Dry Tortugas. Among them were the *Nuestra Señora de Atocha* and *La Margarita*,

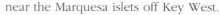

Below:
Divers working on an ancient wreck in the Mediterranean accompanied by a diving bell, which enables them to stay underwater for longer. They can also preserve their oxygen supply by occasionally breathing the air in the bell.

Right:
This gold dish, now on display in Key West, Florida, is part of the fabulous treasure recovered in the 1980s from the Spanish plate vessel Nuestra Señora de Atocha, *which foundered in a hurricane in 1622. The galleon was en route from Havana to Spain when she was wrecked off the Florida Keys.*

near the Marquesa islets off Key West.

Both these vessels were the objects of a 16-year, almost obsessive quest by the American treasure hunter Mel Fisher. His tenacity was rewarded in 1985, when divers located the *Atocha* and reported that she contained precious artifacts, coins, and bullion worth an estimated $450 million, the most valuable haul ever retrieved from a ship of the period. Using side-scanning sonar and suction pipes to clear sand and silt, Fisher's team uncovered a massive pile of silver bars, treasure chests of gold doubloons and silver pieces-of-eight, and exquisite jewelry.

A year after the *Atocha* was lost, two other Spanish galleons also foundered off Florida, near Ais. The *Santissima Trinidad* went down slowly enough for passengers, crew, and cargo to be taken off, but the *Espiritu Santo el Mayor* sank with the loss of all her treasure and 250 lives.

In 1628, the treasure fleets suffered their most humiliating blow, when Dutch warships drove 24 vessels ashore at Matanzas Bay and ransacked most of what they were carrying. And in 1632, a hurricane caused almost equal losses, wrecking 19 galleons along the Mexican coast from the Bajo de las Arcas to Tabasco. In addition to gold and silver, they were carrying cochineal, silk, brazilwood, and indigo.

Two Caribbean wrecks from later in the 17th century show the widely varying successes of salvage divers of the era. The *Nuestra Señora de la Concepción*, another hurricane victim, came to grief on the Silver Bank north of Hispaniola in 1641. About 40 years later, an English expedition financed by King Charles II and led by one William Phips, set about raising her cargo of silver, using a diving bell to create an air pocket from which the divers could breathe. Some 34 tons of treasure were recovered, earning Phips a knighthood and the governship of Massachusetts. By contrast, when the *Nuestra Señora de las Maravillas* collided with another galleon on the Little Bahama Bank, local divers could recover only 1.5 million pesos' worth of the 5 million pesos of treasure. The rest, so far as is known, is still there, covered by the shifting sands.

By the middle of the 18th century, the great days of the Spanish plate fleets were over, and reports of lost treasure tend to involve single ships such as the *Invincible*, struck by lightning in Havana harbor while

carrying a cargo valued at 4 million pesos, and the British warship *Tay*, with treasure to the value of 2 million pesos, which was wrecked on the Alacran Reef off Mexico in 1816. So far as is known, neither has been salvaged.

Treacherous fringes of the Atlantic

The waters of the Caribbean may be a veritable paradise for undersea treasure seekers, but other areas of the Atlantic north of the Equator offer almost as much in lost riches. The margins of the Atlantic, including the English Channel and the North Sea, are a graveyard of shipping — in particular, the eastern seaboard of North America, Ireland, the Orkneys and Shetlands, the Isles of Scilly — and so is the stretch of ocean bounded to the west by the Azores, Madeira, and the Canaries, and to the east by Portugal and Spain.

The last of these is particularly enticing, for it represents the final stage of the voyage for Portuguese vessels returning laden from Brazil and the East Indies, for the survivors of Spanish plate fleets bound from the New World and, later, for British, French, and Dutch merchantmen heading for English Channel and North Sea ports. According to one informed estimate, a small portion of this area — around the mouth of the Guadalquivir River in Spain — contains between 500 and 600 wrecks, few of which have yet been pinpointed, let alone salvaged. Treasures outshining even those of the *Atocha* may be there for the finding.

Between the Iberian peninsula and the Azores, the ocean enjoys an eerie reputation almost equal to that of the Bermuda Triangle. There the first man to sail around the world single-handed, Joshua Slocum, reported that in 1895 his boat had been guided by the ghost of one of Columbus' pilots. There, too, the deserted *Mary Celeste* was discovered in 1872. Although the *Mary Celeste* was not carrying treasure in the normal sense, and indeed her cargo was virtually intact, her lifeboats, navigation books and equipment, and ship's papers were missing, and would be worth a fortune if they were ever found.

The Azores and Madeira were welcome sights to seamen nearing the end of a long Atlantic voyage, but another group of islands, far to the north, presented a hazard that most ships' captains would prefer not to have to face, even today. They are the Scillies, off the southwest tip of England. With the coasts of Devon and Cornwall nearby, they have probably claimed more vessels than any other

Right:
Some of the jewelry found in the wreck of the Nuestra Señora de Atocha.

Far right:
Treasure hunter Mel Fisher proudly displays gold finds from the Atocha.

region of the eastern Atlantic — most dramatically in recent years the oil tanker *Torrey Canyon*, which came to grief on the Seven Stones Reef in 1967. Nowadays, this region is one of the favorite European hunting grounds for both professional and amateur treasure seekers.

In the period from 1641 to 1743, no fewer than seven treasure ships sank off the Scillies, of which the best known is the *Association*, rediscovered in 1967. Four others have also been traced since then. The *Princess Maria*, a Dutch East Indiaman carrying pieces-of-eight and mercury, went down near Silver Carn in 1686; she was extensively plundered at the time, with King James II taking a share of the spoils, but some valuable artifacts remained when she was relocated in 1973.

At the northern end of the British Isles, the Shetlands, with their treacherous reefs called *skerries*, pose as great a threat to shipping as the Scillies do in the south. Until the 19th century, ships other than those plying locally tended to avoid them. However, in some circumstances vessels chose to round Britain by the northerly route rather than risk the English Channel and the Straits of Dover, particularly if they belonged to a nation at war with England or France. That was the course picked by the survivors of the defeated Spanish Armada in 1588.

The rugged coasts of Ireland and Wales are fruitful grounds for treasure hunters. At least six ships from the Armada have been traced off Ireland, leaving perhaps 10 more still to be located. There are also many wrecks along the Irish coast dating from the 19th century, when transatlantic traffic was reaching its peak and

Above:
A cannon and some coins retrieved from a wreck near the Scilly Isles off the southwest tip of Britain.

Right:
The sinking of the unarmed Lusitania *unleashed waves of emotion and hostility on both sides of the Atlantic. The authorities were not above capitalizing on popular feeling to boost enlistment, as this recruiting poster shows.*

many emigrants were seeking a new life in North America.

However, three ships in particular have attracted enormous attention from salvagers in this area. The earliest was the steamship *Royal Charter*, which foundered off Moelfre on the Isle of Anglesey in 1859 while returning from Australia with miners who had made their fortunes in the goldfields there. About 400 people died, many of them trying to swim ashore with their valuables. Coins and jewelry are still being washed up on local beaches. It is generally believed that a substantial amount of bullion is still aboard.

The second is the Cunard liner *Lusitania*, torpedoed in St George's Channel in 1915 in a disaster surpassed in 20th-century maritime lore only by the sinking of the *Titanic*. Out of nearly 2,000 people aboard, 1,198 perished. According to rumor, the *Lusitania* was carrying

gold worth $6 million, but there is no firm evidence of that. Since the late 1960s, salvagers have been working on the wreck and have raised items valued at $4 million, including some of the propellers and the ship's bell, though without finding the gold.

The third is the *Laurentic*, a liner converted into an armed cruiser, sunk by a mine off Lough Swilly in Ireland in 1917. She was carrying gold ingots to Canada to pay for war supplies for Britain. Again, officially, virtually all of the gold was recovered in the years immediately after the wreck.

Coasts of the Americas

The waters from Florida to the mouth of the Orinoco River undoubtedly conceal the biggest concentration of unrecovered undersea treasure in the Americas, and probably the world. However, there are some magnificent prizes

Above:
The development of the aqualung has revolutionized underwater excavation since the 1940s. These divers are working on the wreck of a Spanish vessel off the coast of Cuba.

still awaiting finders elsewhere on both Atlantic and Pacific coasts. Among them are nine ships from the Spanish plate fleet of 1750 which strayed much farther north than was customary. Four went down off Cape Hatteras in North Carolina, and three more off Cape Charles in Virginia, in a hurricane.

Off South Carolina, 160 miles out to sea, the paddle-steamer *Central America* sank during a hurricane in September 1857, with the loss of some 400 lives and Californian gold worth around $1 billion at today's values. Using computer technology and an underwater robot called *Nemo*, a US consortium located the wreck in 1988-89 and began raising its precious cargo 8,000 ft from the seabed. The first stage of the recovery yielded 500 lb of gold in the form of bars, rare 'double eagle' coins and specie privately minted during the California gold rush — 'just like the treasure you've always imagined,' according to recovery team member Judy Conrad.

On the Pacific coast of the Americas, two wrecks in particular are intriguing to treasure-hunters. The Spanish warship *Leocadia* foundered off Punta Santa Elena in Ecuador in 1800 with a large quantity of treasure on board. Much of it was reportedly salvaged at the time, but more is said to await a finder. So far as is known, salvage efforts have been less successful on the paddle-steamer *Golden Gate*, which caught fire and sank near Manzanillo in Mexico in 1862. She was carrying $1.6 million in gold coin, of which little was retrieved.

Waters of the South

In the 17th and 18th centuries, England, France, Holland, and Denmark set up companies to trade with the East Indies, previously the virtual domain of the Portuguese

Right:
Divers at work on the Dutch East Indiaman De Liefde, *wrecked off the Shetland Islands in 1711, reveal a cache of coins amid the wreckage. Efforts were first made to salvage the vessel as long ago as 1712 and are still continuing.*

Left:
Some of the coins recovered from De Liefde. *She was known to have been carrying a fortune in coin and bullion, but little of it has yet been found.*

among the European powers. Their ships plied routes around the Cape of Good Hope and across the Indian Ocean to India itself, the Chinese Empire, the Indonesian islands of Java and Sumatra, Japan, and Australia. As an offshoot of this, a flourishing trade also developed in shipping slaves from Africa to the Americas, in exchange for gold, silver, spices, sugar, and coffee, which were brought back to Europe.

Between 1650 and about 1800, the ships used on the East Indies routes grew dramatically in size, from about 500 tons to 1,000 tons or more. At their peak, these East Indiamen could complete the journey from China to Northern Europe in about 20 months. Unlike their counterparts trading with the Americas, they were more likely to be carrying treasure in the form of gold, silver, and jewels on the outward trip to purchase the spices, porcelain, and tea that they brought home, or to pay those who manned their outposts. To some extent, that changed with the discovery of the Australian goldfields in the mid-19th century.

Australian wrecks

In 1629, several ships belonging to the Dutch

Above:
The Alvin two-man deep-water search and recovery submarine is an example of the advanced technology that is helping salvagers to locate and recover material from open-ocean sites that could not be reached even a few years ago.

Right:
This amphora (wine jar) on the sea bed is encrusted with corals and is the haunt of tropical fish.

East India Company were wrecked on a reef in the Wallabi group of islands, off Western Australia. Among them was the *Batavia*, with a cargo that included jewels and silver coin. Some of the men from the ship took a boat, and what treasure they could salvage, and made for Java, leaving about 250 passengers and crew behind to await their return with a rescue ship. When they eventually got back to the Wallabis, it was to find that a small group had massacred the rest of the party in the hope of carrying off the remaining valuables. The ringleaders were eventually hanged. In 1972, excavation of the *Batavia* began, and items recovered included a large selection of silverware, as well as more than a dozen cannon.

The discovery of the Australian goldfields gave rise to one of the most bizarre stories of

treasure lost at sea in the southern hemisphere, or anywhere else for that matter — the disappearance of the *Starry Crown*. She set sail from Melbourne for London in about 1850, carrying passengers and a ton of Australian gold, only to vanish, presumed lost. Some 20 years later, the whaler *Swordfish* was blown off course and became trapped in Antarctic pack ice. Most of the crew died as their provisions dwindled. Soon, only five were left alive.

As *Swordfish* shifted in the ice, another trapped ship came into view. Two of the *Swordfish* crew, one of them the second mate, Last, went on board and found the mystery ship was the *Starry Crown*, deserted, with most of its boats gone, but with plenty of provisions — and the gold intact. Having no means of moving the gold, Last left it where it was. Eventually, he was rescued with the other

members of the crew, all of whom died on the voyage back to Melbourne, leaving Last the sole possessor of the secret. He eventually shared it with a man called Manton, and together they plotted a return to Antarctica aboard Manton's ship, the *Black Dog*. She too became trapped in the ice and sank, drowning the crew. Manton and Last jumped onto an ice floe and eventually reached the *Starry Crown*, still intact with her gold. Then, according to Last, Manton went mad and attacked his partner, who shot him in what he claimed was self-defense. Last, without the gold, managed to reach open water and was rescued by a whaler, leaving the *Starry Crown* and her precious cargo in the ice's firm grip, perhaps for ever.

Above:

Beneath its tourist brochure sky and sea, the Caribbean is perhaps the world's richest underwater treasure store.

The 1715 plate fleet

For more than 200 years, the Spanish conquerors of the New World systematically plundered their transatlantic territories, shipping vast quantities of gold, silver, and other precious materials back to their perennially impoverished homeland. Between about 1552 and 1648, three convoys or plate fleets a year made the hazardous journey from the Spanish Main. The ships were laden to the gunwales with treasure, including silver from the mines at Potosí, in what is now Bolivia.

The plate fleets were a natural target for Spain's enemies, in particular England and

Right:
Former building contractor Kip Wagner, president of Real Eight salvage, with some of the treasure from La Holandesa, *one of the wrecks of the Spanish plate fleet of 1715.*

Holland, and for freebooting pirates owing allegiance to no nation. However, they were escorted by fighting galleons, and nine out of every ten treasure ships managed to get through. Their worst enemy was the treacherous weather of the Caribbean, where shallow waters and hurricanes at certain times of the year combine to create conditions that are a deathtrap for heavily laden and cumbersome sailing vessels. Many foundered between Florida, the Bahamas, and Bermuda, their last safe anchorage in the New World.

A fortune fathoms deep

One of the biggest single disasters to befall a Spanish plate fleet occurred in July 1715, when a 12-ship convoy left Havana in Cuba carrying 6.5 million pesos (at then-current values) in gold and silver bullion and coin, and the equivalent amount in contraband smuggled aboard by the crew in defiance of the death penalty which was the punishment for such actions in Spain. The fleet consisted of five ships from the New Spanish flota (fleet), a further six Spanish ships from Panama, and one French vessel. In addition to bullion and coin, they carried cocoa, brazilwood, vanilla, tortoiseshell, pearls, jewelry, tobacco, hides, and rare Chinese porcelain.

Six days out of Havana, in the Straits of Florida, the fleet was struck by a hurricane. All but the French ship sank, with the loss of more than 1,000 lives, although 1,500 people survived. The Spaniards were quick to try to retrieve their loss. Within six months they had set up a salvage camp near Sebastian in Florida and engaged nearly 300 Indians to dive to the wrecks. Within four years, the divers recovered most of the treasure.

That satisfied the Spaniards, and the circumstances in which the plate fleet foundered were largely forgotten, to the extent that later historians disagreed over where the disaster had taken place. They proposed two sites, 200 miles apart and both wrong. In reality, the wrecks were spread over 50 miles from Cape Canaveral to 5 miles south of Fort Pierce Inlet.

Left:
Shifting sand and dune grass near Cape Canaveral, Florida, part of the coast along which the Spanish plate fleet was struck by a hurricane in July 1715.

Wagner hits the jackpot

It was not until 1948, when a Florida building contractor called Kip Wagner discovered seven silver coins on the beach at Sebastian, that the treasure once again exerted its lure. Wagner worked in secret, combing the archives for references to the loss of the fleet and observing the action of wind and waves on the Florida coastline. He reasoned that the location of the Spanish salvage base would provide the key to that of the wrecks, and he found it near Sebastian with the aid of a mine-detector. His research showed that the base had been raided while the Spaniards were still trying to raise the treasure — perhaps by English freebooters.

Wagner's persistence paid off. In 1959, he partly lifted his veil of secrecy, engaging amateur divers to help pinpoint the wrecks. He found seven or eight of them (the exact details are still shrouded in mystery), established legal title to the relics, and created a museum in which the finds could be displayed.

Prominent among them was a gold whistle on a golden chain of 2,176 links, the insignia of a Spanish fleet commander. Within the whistle, shaped as a dragon, was a solid gold toothpick, which prompted Wagner to comment: 'What kind of dinner can a man eat to pick his teeth with that?' It has been valued at up to $60,000.

Wagner recovered Spanish pieces-of-eight — more than 1,000 in one day alone — and individual and fire-fused silver coins. There were also 28 undamaged Chinese porcelain vases and an authentic treasure chest, a wooden box 3 x 1 x 1 feet in size, crammed with 3,000 silver coins.

So far as is known, three or four wrecks from the 1715 plate fleet still remain to be located in the Straits of Florida.

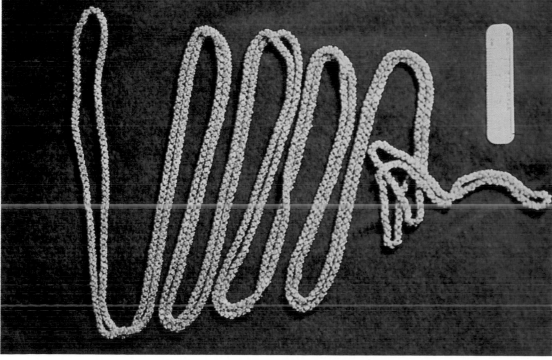

Above:
A diver works on the wreck of a Spanish galleon off the Florida coast. Altogether, 11 treasure ships foundered there in 1715 and at least three of them have still to be found.

Left:
This gold chain and whistle was part of the insignia of a Spanish fleet commander. It is just one of the priceless artifacts recovered from ships of the 1715 plate fleet lost off the Florida coast near Sebastian.

Red gold of the Arctic

The Barents Sea, north of Norway and inside the Arctic Circle, produces some of the worst conditions faced by sailors anywhere around the globe — temperatures that can drop to 30°F below zero and tearing winds that lash the waters to a frenzy, coating superstructures with thick layers of ice and snow. Even in peacetime it is no place for the faint-hearted; during World War II, when the threats of enemy submarines, surface ships, and aircraft were added to the natural hazards, it was an icy hell on earth.

From 1941, when Hitler's Germany invaded the Soviet Union, the Barents Sea became a theater of water. The beleaguered Russians were desperate for weapons, aircraft, tanks, and all the other materiel of conflict from their new allies, the United States and Britain. The main supply route lay through the Barents Sea, to the ice-free northern Russian port of Murmansk, and along it steamed convoy after convoy to stiffen the Russians' resistance. In 1942 alone, some 1.7 million tons of equipment were sea-freighted to Murmansk; about 275,000 tons were lost on the way, with dozens of ships and hundreds of men.

The ill-fated convoy QP11

The Russians paid for their armaments in

nothing less than gold bullion. On 25th April 1942, the British cruiser *Edinburgh* loaded aboard 465 ingots, packed five at a time into cheap wooden cases, part of the reimbursement to the United States. The cases were described as ship's stores and stowed in the bomb-room. With her precious cargo — worth about $62 million at today's values — the ship sailed north along Kola Inlet toward the open sea, ostensibly just another escort vessel for the returning Murmansk convoy QP11. The *Edinburgh* was some 15 miles ahead of the convoy when a German submarine struck, firing three torpedoes that partially crippled her but left her afloat. She

attempted to limp back to the main body of QP11, with protection from two other British warships. However, the Germans had not finished, launching three destroyers into the fray in addition to the submarines. During the battle, the *Edinburgh* was again torpedoed, in the early morning of 2nd May. Still she did not sink, although heavily damaged and with 57 of her 700 men dead.

The survivors were taken off by the escort ships for the return to Murmansk. Rear-Admiral Stuart Bonham-Carter, in overall charge of the convoy, then took the decision to scuttle the gallant *Edinburgh* so that she and her cargo should not fall into enemy hands. At 6.30 pm,

Above:

The gallant cruiser Edinburgh *endured three days of enemy attack and several direct hits by torpedo in the icy waters of the Barents Sea in 1942, but remained afloat. Eventually she was sunk by her own side to prevent her cargo of gold bullion from falling into German hands. All but 34 of her gold ingots were eventually recovered in 1981.*

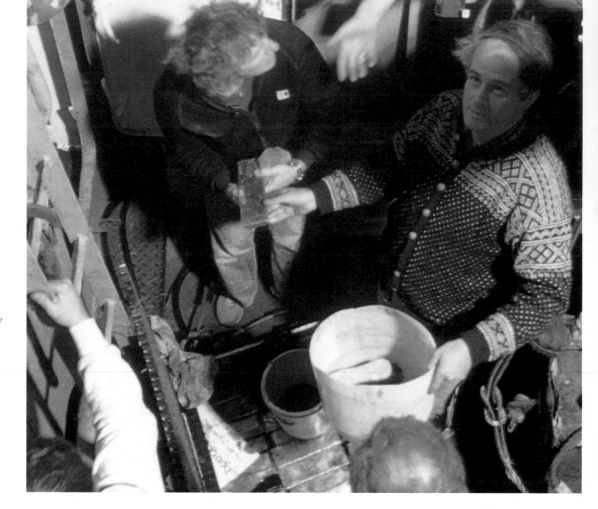

Right:
Aboard the Stephaniturm, *the advanced recovery vessel used to salvage the* Edinburgh's *gold. Throughout the dive, the atmosphere was lighthearted, but a joke in bad taste, in which a lamp was left inside a skull on the wreck to frighten the next diving team, temporarily soured the atmosphere.*

the escorting destroyer *Foresight* fired a torpedo into her hull. The *Edinburgh* rolled over and slipped beneath the icy waters, to what seemed an inaccessible grave more than 800 ft down.

Stormy salvage

There she rested undisturbed for nearly 40 years, but the lure of gold and the advance of technology meant that she was not destined to remain in peace for ever. Keith Jessop, a Yorkshireman who had wide experience as a diver both in salvage and on North Sea oil rigs, became obsessed with the *Edinburgh*. After years of research and an abortive attempt to trace the wreck, he struck a deal with the Aberdeen diving contractors Wharton-Williams to help in raising the gold.

Matters were not simple. The *Edinburgh* had been declared a British war grave, restricting access to it. Other salvage companies were also interested in obtaining permission to dive for the wreck. And the Soviet Union,

which had a partial claim on the gold, was suspicious about Jessop's plans. Eventually, the difficulties were smoothed over, the contracts signed, and the exact position of the *Edinburgh* traced by a combination of sonar and underwater video. All was set for the gold hunt to begin in the fall of 1981.

For the recovery attempt, Wharton-Williams, who were mainly responsible for the technical side of the operation, employed a recovery vessel called the *Stephaniturm*. From this floating base, 12 divers, working in pairs and using a diving bell, descended to the wreck. They dived from 17th September to 7th October and managed to find in the cold, murky waters 431 of the 465 ingots.

The salvage of the *Edinburgh* was at the time the deepest ever carried out. It yielded $56 million, of which $20 million went to the Soviet Union, and $11 million to the British government. Of the remaining $25 million, 90 percent went to Wharton-Williams and just 10 percent to Keith Jessop.

Left:
Mission accomplished — some of the gold ingots bearing Russian casting marks recovered from the Edinburgh in 20 days of concentrated relay diving in Arctic waters. Altogether, the gold retrieved was worth $56 million.

The pride of monarchs

From the middle of the 15th century, Europe's maritime powers began building vast floating fortresses to support their conventional shipping in times of war. These huge vessels were not intended to stay at sea for long — generally, they never ventured more than about 24 hours' sailing from a friendly port — so they were not subject to the constraints of design and construction that applied to smaller galleons plying the open oceans in search of new sources of wealth.

The monarchs of Europe vied with each other in building such leviathans. In 1418, Henry V of England's pride was the *Grace Dieu*, which displaced 1,400 tons (until around 1600, the biggest galleons were no more than 600 tons). Henry VIII's *Harry Grace à Dieu* was 1,000 tons. The vessels were cumbersome enough because of their weight, and their fitters made matters worse by cramming them with as much cannon as possible to create intimidating fire-power.

Unfortunately for those who manned such ships, this left them top-heavy and vulnerable in all but the calmest conditions. Several sank in weather that would hardly have troubled conventional galleons — among them, England's *Mary Rose* and the Swedish *Wasa*, the objects of two of the most remarkable underwater salvage operations of recent times.

The fall and rise of the *Mary Rose*

The *Mary Rose* was relatively light for a floating fortress, just 600 tons. But she had been designed originally as a conventional warship, and then enlarged and refitted to carry 60 guns. To accommodate the cannon, gun-ports had been cut into the sides of the hull — an innovation in the mid-16th century.

On 18th June 1545, the *Mary Rose* was riding at anchor in Portsmouth harbor. waiting to do battle with the French. Suddenly, as the result of a stiff breeze, she heeled over and, to the horror of the onlookers, who included Henry VIII, sank, drowning all but about 50 of the 700 men on board. The gun-ports had been left open and water rushing through them probably contributed to the swiftness of the disaster.

Below:
A 16th-century manuscript now in Magdalene College, Cambridge, lists the armaments of the Mary Rose, *pride of England's battle fleet in the reign of King Henry VIII. Wrecked in harbor by a freak gust of wind, she lay buried in mud until archaeologists began excavating her in 1973.*

For more than 400 years, the *Mary Rose* lay at the bottom of Portsmouth harbor, until she was relocated under 15 feet of mud by divers in 1965. From 1973 onward, archaeologists worked on the wreck, eventually raising a substantial portion of the timber hull. As a fighting ship, the *Mary Rose* was not carrying treasure of the conventional kind, but she yielded a vast array of artifacts — including weapons, musical instruments, and the personal possessions of crew members, some of which are unique.

The fate of the *Wasa*

If the loss of the *Mary Rose* was a humiliation for Henry VIII, that of the *Wasa* was an even bigger one for King Gustavus II of Sweden. In the 1620s, the Swedes knew little about building large warships, so they hired a Dutchman to design one for them. The result was a square-rigger 180 ft long with a displacement of 1,400 tons and two continuous gun-decks with ports, carrying cannon weighing a total of 71 tons. As befitted the

pride of the Swedish navy, she had an elaborately sculptured superstructure reminiscent of a castle. That, and the cannon, gave her a dangerously high center of gravity.

In August 1628, the *Wasa* set off on her maiden voyage. But she had hardly left her moorings when she, like the *Mary Rose*, was caught by a sudden gust of wind. She immediately heeled over and sank, off the island of Beckholmen in Stockholm, at the approaches to the open waters of the Baltic.

The wreck was relocated in the 1950s, using a core-sampler, a device for obtaining specimens of the sea bottom for analysis. The *Wasa* was raised in 1959. The timbers were in a remarkably good state of preservation, because destructive creatures such as ship-worms are not very active in cold northern waters. The artifacts, too, were in good condition, and included cannon, coins, cooking pots, and clothing belonging to the crew.

Above:
A view of the deck of the restored Swedish warship Wasa. *Having capsized and sunk in Stockholm harbor on her maiden voyage in 1628, the vessel was raised in 1959 and is now preserved in a special air-conditioned building.*

Death of a battle fleet

Below:
The English fleet that challenged the might of the Spanish Armada had fewer ships and men than the enemy — but nearly twice the number of cannon. Daring seamanship by English captains such as Drake, Hawkins, and Frobisher left the Spanish outmaneuvered, and fireships broke up the Armada's close formation. Even so, only about 25 Spanish ships were lost during engagements; as many again perished trying to round the western coast of the British Isles.

The Spanish Armada, the vanguard of Phillip II's attempt to crush England in 1588, was the mightiest battle fleet the world had yet seen, a massive display of sea power consisting of 30,000 men and 1,000 cannon aboard 24 galleons, 40 armed merchantmen, and 36 smaller vessels, supported by 25 supply ships. After two weeks of running fights against the English navy, which was outnumbered though not outgunned and was led by veteran privateers such as Hawkins and Drake, the Armada was still a formidable force of more than 100 ships.

But adverse winds and the depredations of the English had left the Spaniards without the stomach to continue the battle. On 2nd August, off the coast of Scotland, their commander, the Duke of Medina Sidonia, issued his orders. The fleet was to head back to Spain, not through the English Channel where the enemy could once more attack, but round Cape Wrath in the north of Scotland and the west of Ireland — a route for which his captains did not have charts. This handicap would not have mattered if all the ships had obeyed instructions and stayed well offshore. But some, desperate for food and fresh water, ventured onto the wild west Irish coast, where they were wrecked and their crews drowned or slaughtered.

Wrecks galore

Altogether, between 20 and 25 vessels were lost in Medina's retreat, in addition to about the same number captured or sunk in the earlier fighting. The search for the wrecks, and the treasure that at least some of them carried, continues to fascinate many people. Those wrecks that have been located — though not all salvaged — are scattered over a wide area. *El Gran Grifón* went down in Stroms Hellier, off Fair Isle in the Shetlands. The *Duque de Florencia* perished in Tobermory Bay, Scotland. *La Trinidad Valencera* sank in the Bay of Kinnagoe. Off the Irish coast, the *Girona* was wrecked on the Bunboyes Rock,

Left:
The tranquil waters of Tobermory Bay in Scotland reputedly conceal treasures worth anything up to $100 million. The main paychest of the Spanish Armada was reputedly aboard a galleon variously called the Duque di Florencia, *the* Florida *or the* San Francisco, *which sank in the bay after the Armada's defeat in 1588. Some say the vessel was blown up by a Scottish prisoner taken by the crew following an argument with local clansmen over payment for food and water. Others maintain she was sunk by the spell of a local witch, Gromshuil Mhor of Lochaber. The site has drawn treasure seekers since 1640; later in the 17th century, the Duke of Argyll brought a diving bell from Sweden to try to trace the wreck. Learning of the Duke's attempts and eager to claim the gold for himself, King Charles II sent a warship to stop the operation. The Duke took the matter to court and won sole rights of salvage, which his successors still maintain. But the most impressive relic so far found is a bronze cannon, attributed to the Italian sculptor Benvenuto Cellini.*

off Antrim, three wrecks have been traced in Streedagh Bay in Sligo, and the *Santa Maria de la Rosa* foundered on Great Blasquet Island near the Dingle Peninsula. The *San Pedro Mayor* successfully rounded Scotland and Ireland, only to be blown ashore near Hope Cove in Devon. So it is possible that further Armada ships may lie almost anywhere along the western coasts of the British Isles.

Treasure lost and found

Rumors of treasure carried by the Armada began to grow even before the fleet was finally defeated. They were fed by a prize taken by Francis Drake. In the midst of battle, Drake took time off to escort the Spanish galleon *Nuestra Señora del Rosario* ashore in Dorset, and to help himself to the 55,000 ducats she was carrying. Legends of Spanish treasure abound on the Irish coast, and it is possible that local inhabitants pillaged the more accessible wrecks as soon as they could.

The diver Archibald Miller worked on the *Florencia* in the 17th century, but it was not until the 1960s that full-scale attempts began at salvaging the remnants of the Armada. The

Belgian Robert Sténuit searched for the *Girona* off Antrim in Ireland.

In 1967, Sténuit found the site, retrieving pieces-of-eight, an anchor, and a gold chain. The following year, he returned with better equipment and discovered a whole collection of magnificent items, now on display in the Ulster Museum in Belfast. Among them were more than 400 gold coins, some 800 silver coins, and precious jewelry set with gems, including a brooch depicting a salamander, and a gold box in which holy relics were carried.

The *Girona* finds are not necessarily typical. The ship, which was Italian even though it sailed with the Armada, had taken aboard the valuables from two other wrecked vessels before foundering herself. Nevertheless, contemporary records show that the Armada *was* a floating treasure store as well as a battle fleet. The prospects of such riches are more than enough to keep the quest for the Armada wrecks alive. However, even when a ship is located, disappointment may follow. The *Santa Maria de la Rosa*, found in 1968, yielded only two pewter plates, a medallion, and a handful of gold and silver coins.

Wreck ahoy

Storms, winds, rip tides, rocks, and enemy vessels have been perils of the sea since man first took to the waters more than 9,000 years ago. But of all the dangers threatening seafarers until the 19th century, none were more feared and loathed than wreckers — men and women living in coastal villages who supplemented their incomes by deliberately luring passing ships to disaster and plundering them.

The south and east coasts of Britain, from Cape Cornwall to Cape Wrath in the north of Scotland, were notorious wreckers' havens in the 18th century. So was the west coast of Ireland, where the populations of entire villages conspired to defy the law and ransack foundered ships. Across the Atlantic, Nova Scotians and New Englanders practiced wrecking, inspiring one of the most enduring legends of the sea, that of the *Palatine*. The vessel was said to have been lured onto the rocks on the west coast of Block Island, off Rhode Island, by wreckers' lanterns on the night of 27th December 1738, and set ablaze

Below and right:
A British Navy salvage team near Gilstone Rocks off the Scilly Isles, where the treasure-laden ship Association *came to grief in 1707. The wreck lies about 60 ft down, between the inner and outer rocks, in an area where dozens of vessels have gone to their doom.*

after its cargo had been pillaged.

At their most harmless, wreckers were simply beachcombers, benefitting, albeit in macabre fashion, from the misfortunes befalling ships off the shores where they lived. But many took an active part in shaping events, dousing or moving warning lights, or indulging in the practice called 'jibber the kibber' or 'Judas lights', in which lanterns were hung at night from the necks of grazing animals to confuse unwary navigators.

Among the wreckers' most notorious feats was the ransacking of the tea clipper *Gossamer* off Chivelstone in Devon, England, in December 1868. On passage to Adelaide, she was beset by bad weather in the English Channel and, handicapped by a pilot who was later found to be drunk, sailed too close to the coast and broke up on the rocks. Before the police and militia could arrive, local wreckers had stripped her of most of her cargo.

The wreck of the *Association*

Wreckers played a grisly role, too, in the loss of the *Association* and four other ships of the British Mediterranean fleet off the Isles of Scilly in October 1707. The fleet, under the command of Admiral Sir Cloudesley Shovell, was carrying $3 million in bullion and silver, mostly the property of Portuguese merchants sending it to England for safe keeping. Despite the warning of a seaman who was hanged from the mast

for insubordination, Shovell believed he was close to Brittany rather than over the Outer Gilstone Rock in an area where many other vessels had been wrecked. All five vessels foundered, with the loss of some 2,000 lives. Shovell himself is believed to have reached the beach alive, but to have been strangled or suffocated by local women eager to steal his personal jewelry.

The subsequent history of the *Association* is a tale of mystery and bureaucratic bungling. In a map dating from 1740, the reef on which the ship was wrecked is referred to as Shovell Rock, but the name was later changed, perhaps by locals anxious to obscure the exact location and to plunder the treasure for themselves. Alternatively, the powerful Godolphin family, lords of the Isles of Scilly from 1571, may have ordered the name change and suppressed evidence so they could loot the wrecks and avoid having to hand the contents over to the British Crown.

A salvage free-for-all

In 1967, a diving team from the Royal Navy — titular owners of the *Association* and its cargo — relocated the wreck. But underwater recovery was still in its infancy and few ground rules had been laid down for the way in which it was carried out. From the outset, the find, which included gold and silver coins and bronze cannon, was widely publicized and two other teams, in addition to the Royal Navy, were in possession of valid licenses to dive to the wreck.

Other treasure hunters were less scrupulous about the rules, with the result that at one stage there were no fewer than five teams salvaging the *Association*, together with a shifting population of freelance divers who switched allegiance from one group to another, or foraged on their own account. Few bothered to declare their finds, knowing that if they did so the British Crown would claim at least half of the value. One educated estimate puts the treasure recovered at nearly $1 million, or about one-third of the original cargo, most of it finding its way into private hands. That implies that a further $2 million may still lie in the vicinity of the Gilstone Rock. But no one knows how much may have been retrieved secretly by the wreckers of Scilly over the past 250 years, either on their own behalf or acting for their masters, the Godolphins.

Far left:
A skull from the Association *is a grim reminder of the perils of the sea — not only wind and waves, but the activities of pirates, wreckers, and other cut-throats. These and many other items were raised from the* Association *in 1967.*

Below:
This dramatic seascape by P. J. de Loutherberg (1740–1812) shows that victims of a shipwreck had more to contend with than simply getting ashore safely. Wreckers do battle with the survivors as they beach their lifeboat, to remove witnesses of the crime and to rob them of their personal belongings. The picture is in Southampton Art Gallery, England.

Raise the *Titanic*

Below:
Two artist's reconstructions of
the sinking of the Titanic *painted*
from descriptions given by
survivors.

No shipwreck of modern times has so captured the popular imagination as that of the *Titanic*, the allegedly unsinkable pride of the White Star Line of Liverpool, England. Holed by an iceberg on the night of 14th-15th April 1912, on her maiden voyage, the luxurious 52,310-ton liner foundered in 13,000 ft of water some 560 miles off Cape Race, Newfoundland, with the loss of 1,513 lives. Among those who perished were no fewer than ten American millionaires, including John Jacob Astor and Benjamin Guggenheim.

For decades, finding and raising the *Titanic* was the dream of treasure hunters the world over. In the late summer of 1985, part of that dream came true. A joint French-American team of scientists experimenting with underwater surveying equipment pinpointed and filmed the wreck. Their achievement immediately unleashed controversy — between those who believed the liner should have been left undisturbed as a marine grave and those who argued that she should be raised; and between those who maintained that the feat of salvaging the ship from the depths of the North Atlantic was technically possible, and those who contended that it was not.

Salvage claims

One of the scientists associated with the original discovery, Robert Ballard, was in no doubt. He declared that any attempt at salvage would be 'ridiculous'. But Robert Marx, a leading treasure salvager, felt the task could be partially accomplished by using robots and explosives, while conceding it resembled 'Mission Impossible'. 'No one has ever found anything that deep,' he pointed out.

At the same time, another salvager, John Pierce, won a legal victory in the British High Court which, he asserted, made raising the *Titanic*, at an estimated cost of up to $4 billion, a viable proposition. The court ruled that Pierce and his colleagues were entitled to keep items salvaged from the liner *Lusitania*, torpedoed in 1915. Pierce maintained that the decision implied that the *Titanic* and her contents belonged to whoever managed to salvage them, rather than to the successors of the White Star Line or to the insurers who had

Left:
The mighty Titanic *undergoing sea trials in Belfast Lough after completion at the Northern Ireland shipyard of Harland & Wolff and before her ill-fated maiden voyage from Southampton in 1912. The hull and fixtures were insured for £1 million, the risk spread among some 70 insurance companies and Lloyds of London syndicates.*

paid out on the original loss. But many English legal experts questioned Pierce's reasoning.

Lost fortune

Another controversy is over the valuables that the *Titanic*'s predominantly wealthy passengers were reputedly carrying with them when the vessel sank. Some people believe that a fortune in jewelry awaits the first salvagers to reach the wreck, and that one victim — a diamond merchant — had deposited uncut stones to the value of $7 million in the ship's vault.

Most experts discount such stories, but their reasons for doing so conflict, leaving optimistic treasure hunters with a glimmer of hope. One school of thought holds that wealthy voyagers like the Astors and the Guggenheims did not take their real jewelry with them, but travelled with paste imitations. Another cites the ship's manifest of items lodged with the purser for safekeeping; that amounted to no more than half a page, with no single item valued at more than $500 or so. The highest insurance claim lodged after the disaster was $174,000 by a female passenger who had lost most of her wardrobe. And, said witnesses to the event, first-class travellers collected their easily portable possessions before the liner finally went down.

Two valuable items are, however, known to have been on the *Titanic* — a painting by Blondel called 'La Circasienne au Bain', valued in 1912 at $100,000, and a luxuriously bound and illustrated copy of the *Rubaiyat*, by Omar Khayyam. More than 70 years' immersion in the cold waters of the Atlantic is hardly likely to have improved either of them.

Salvager Robert Marx believes that the stories of fabulous collections of jewelry are largely irrelevant. 'Each tea cup is going to be worth a fortune,' he says.

Above:
Shocked office workers in London learn that the unthinkable has happened and the unsinkable has sunk in April 1912. The unique double hull of the Titanic *was supposed to give her all the protection needed against the treacherous North Atlantic.*

Right and far right:
Three of more than 12,000 underwater photographs taken of the wreck of the Titanic *when she was located in September 1985. The pictures were shot from cameras on the Argo, a prototype underwater robot sled intended for use in the US Navy's submarine warfare programme. The Argo can stay submerged for weeks on end and roam miles of the deep seabed, feeding back television pictures and other data to scientists aboard a mother ship. The mission that traced the* Titanic *— jointly conducted by the Woods Hole Oceanographic Institution of the USA and France's Institute for Research and Exploitation of the Sea — chose to search for the vessel to demonstrate the Argo's ability 'to find something that no one else could find'.*

These pictures show anchor chains, winches and capstans on the ship's bow deck, and part of her deck railing.

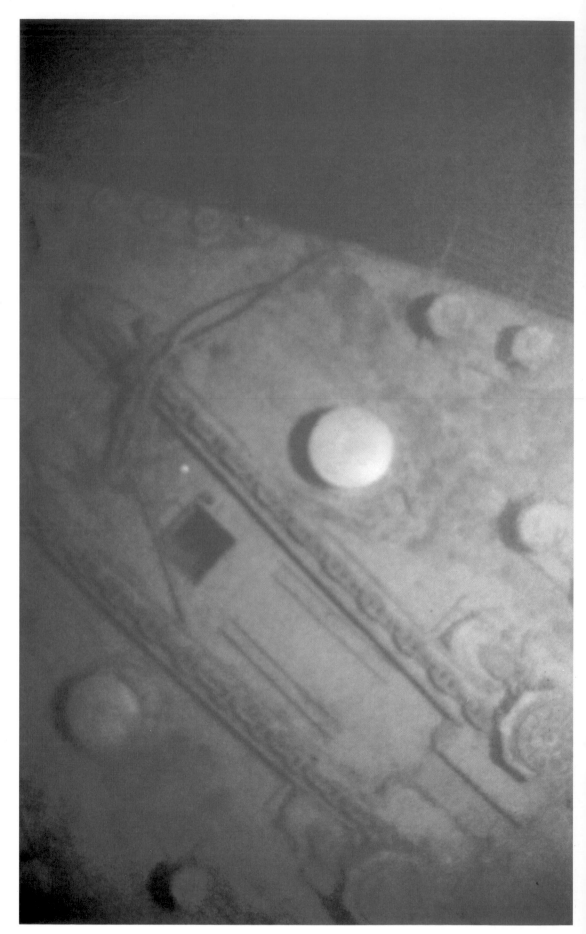

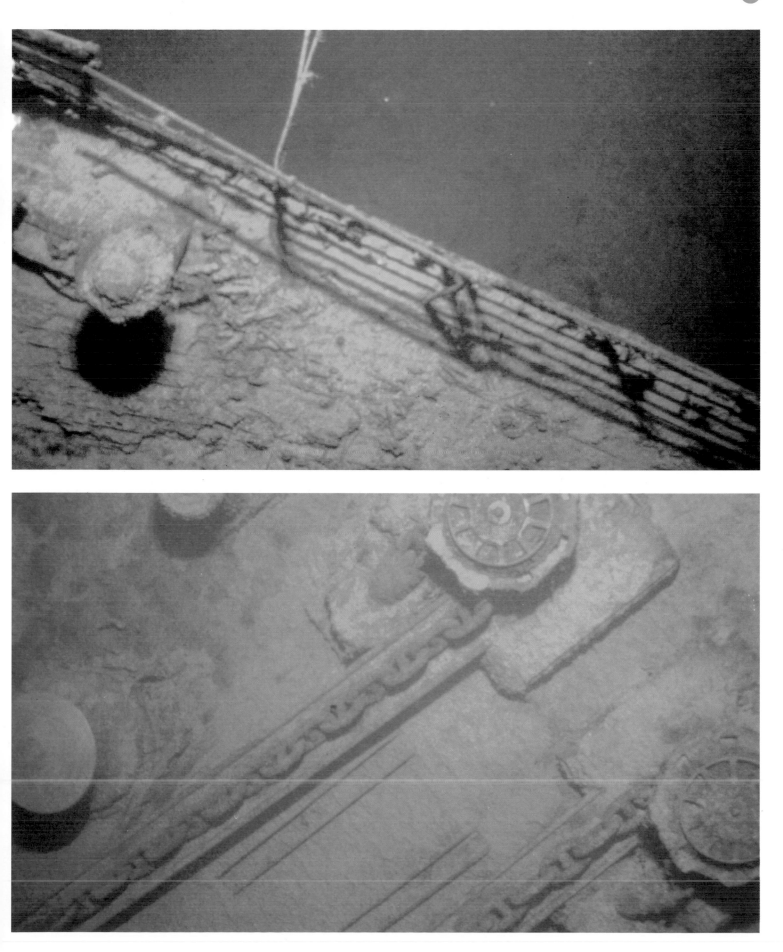

3

Riches from the Earth

If there is one theme that has been guaranteed to excite treasure hunters across the ages it is that of legendary 'lost riches': forgotten cities concealing the wealth of ancient tribes, abandoned mines rich in gold, silver, or precious stones, hidden hoards, and unclaimed caches. Usually such stories follow something of a pattern, involving a lost explorer or sole survivor, convinced of the value of a find, yet curiously unable to retrace his steps to find it again. They are often tied to tantalizingly specific locations, with just enough verifiable fact mixed in among the legends and half-truths to make them seem feasible. Paradoxically, the very fact that the hidden treasures have never been found, instead of discouraging seekers, only adds to their fascination.

The lure of El Dorado
Historically, the greatest, most exhaustive and yet least successful quest for fabulous riches was the Spanish search for El Dorado. When the conquistadores arrived in the New World in the 16th century, they came with a crucifix in one hand and a sword in the other. They encountered remarkable native cultures quite outside the European experience, yet evinced no particular interest in them.

Within scarcely half a century, they destroyed three ancient cultures — Aztec, Maya, and Inca. Native populations who managed to survive the sword were cut down by European diseases. Ancient religions were rooted out and persecuted, cultural practices erased. All the Spaniards wanted was loot, and that they took in prodigious quantities. So much so that they were reluctant to believe that the sources of supply were depleted by their first hauls — although Atahualpa's golden ransom can scarcely have left much in the Inca treasury. The Spaniards were convinced that there was more, and still more, to be found. Much, they believed, was deliberately hidden from them. And when they had tracked down and ransacked that, they began to listen to rumors of fabulously wealthy peoples living just beyond their reach. So began the quest for El Dorado, that mirage conjured by gold-fevered brains. Expedition after expedition sought it, many men losing their lives in the process, for El Dorado was never more than a tantalizing myth.

And yet, in time, the image of Inca gold, or Aztec gold, became mixed up with lost Spanish gold, until the whole American continent south of Arizona and Texas became a possible source of lost treasure belonging to someone or other.

It is interesting that many of the stories of lost treasure from the southern United States include references to long-dead Spaniards. They have continued to fascinate, through the 19th century up to the present day. Just occasionally, dramatic archaeological or historical finds turn up to give them credibility. The fantastic stories of cities buried beneath the jungles of Central America led Stephens and Catherwood to the temples of the Maya in the 1840s, and Thompson to the ceremonial well at Chichén Itzá, with its priceless haul.

Colonel Fawcett's expeditions

If the Maya could be rediscovered after 300 years, might there not have been other civilizations 'lost' in the impenetrable rain forests of, say, Brazil? The British explorer Colonel Percy Fawcett certainly thought so. He had heard the story of the 'Lost Mines of the Muribeca', a tale of fabulous wealth in the mountains several hundred miles from the coast of Brazil, once exploited by a Portuguese half-caste in the 17th century. In 1753, a strong Portuguese expedition had set off in search of the mines. It was away for ten years, and returned with a detailed account of its adventures, which described finding the mines near a waterfall in a range of white crystal mountains not far from a mysterious and deserted ancient city. Many have since tried to find the mines. In 1921, Fawcett set off alone to find them and, after wandering through the jungle for three months, claimed to have found the lost city. He made another expedition in 1925, but was never seen again. Even today some parts of the area covered by his expeditions remain largely unmapped, and it is just possible something may one day be found there. If so, it will not be the fabled wealth of the Muribeca which will cause a sensation, but the evidence of an unknown civilization in an area long insisted by archaeologists to be without one.

Above:
Colonel Percy Harrison Fawcett, British gentleman explorer. He was one of many adventurers lured by stories of lost treasures deep in the South American jungle. Fawcett claimed that he had seen the 'Lost Mines of the Muribeca', but was never able to prove it. He disappeared while on an expedition in Brazil in 1925.

Left:
This priceless and breathtakingly beautiful ear-lobe ring from Ecuador is typical of the riches the conquistadores looted from the Americas. The hope of finding forgotten caches inspired many a treasure hunter well into the 20th century.

Above:

The conquistadores were the greatest despoilers in history, ruthlessly sacking one country after another. This pyramid at Teotihuacán in Mexico is a dramatic memorial to a lost world destroyed by the lust for gold.

African and American caches

It was, perhaps, inevitable that during the 19th century, that great age of discovery, many adventurers motivated by the desire to find legendary lost tribes, towns, and treasures. During the great European race to explore and colonize Africa, many men were drawn by tales which turned out to be pure moonshine. Africa, south of the Sahara, proved disappointing for those keen to find lost treasures. When Cecil Rhodes conquered Rhodesia in the 1890s, he was seeking to duplicate the successful diamond and gold discoveries at Kimberley and Johannesburg. He believed the great stone circles of the Zimbabwe ruins, and their associated gold workings, to be the Ophir of the Bible. But all Rhodesia brought him were costly wars with the native inhabitants, the Matabele (Ndebele) and Mashona, and disillusion. The ruins of Great Zimbabwe produced only a handful of treasure, and in trying to find the non-existent ancient race that supposedly built the great stone circles, the excavators destroyed most of the evidence of the real Africans who had.

Lost mines, however, continue to hold a fascination. The most famous story concerns the Lost Dutchman mine, which still draws optimistic treasure hunters to the area of Weaver's Needle in the Superstition Mountains outside Phoenix, Arizona. Yet the Lost Dutchman is just one of several similar stories about abandoned mine workings or hidden caches. With their dramatic stories straight out of a Western, and a geography so harsh that it is easy to believe that anything might remain hidden up an overgrown canyon, beneath a rockfall, or under a tangle of mesquite, it is hard for anyone bitten by the treasure hunting bug to resist them.

One thing is certain: there are still plenty of tales of buried treasure to keep potential seekers enthralled for years to come. Many are probably pure myth, and will continue to exert their fascination simply because there is nothing to be found. But there is enough truth behind some to suggest that, with the aid of modern technology, some lucky and persistent adventurer will one day come across some remarkable and exciting finds.

Left:
The remarkable Aztec calendar stone, proof of the Central American Indians' extraordinary astronomical knowledge. But the conquistadores were not interested in art or learning; they smashed idols and destroyed codices in an attempt to eradicate religions considered pagan and barbarian, and ornaments of precious metal were melted down for their bullion value. Onward, Christian soldiers!

Left:
This 17th-century German illustration captures something of the Spanish dream of the search for El Dorado; a conquistador riding a llama is laden with bags of treasure. In reality, few expeditions were this successful.

Schliemann's Troy

There is more than a little romance to the story of Troy. There is Homer's epic poem, of course: the story of the beautiful Helen, kidnapped by the Trojan Paris and rescued at the cost of a ten-year war that ended only when the Trojans were deceived by the Greeks' wooden horse. But modern Troy has its romance, too, in the story of the man who struggled to prove that Homer was dealing in fact rather than myth and that Troy was a real city. That man was Heinrich Schliemann.

Schliemann was born in the village of Neubuckow in eastern Germany in 1822. If we are to believe his own account — and by his own admission Schliemann was quite happy to embroider the truth to make a better story — he first became interested in Troy when he was given an illustrated book on the subject as a child. Certainly by the time he had made his fortune trading in Russia and America, he had both the time and the money to indulge his interests, and Troy was foremost among them.

Although Homer was quite specific about the location of Troy — on the edge of the plain of the Scamander River, across from the Hellespont, or, in other words, opposite the Gallipoli peninsula in modern Turkey — most scholars considered his story mere legend. In addition, archaeology itself was in its infancy. When Schliemann set out to discover Troy in 1870, he was forced to make up his techniques as he went along.

A spectacular dig

Schliemann was convinced by an English enthusiast, Frank Calvert, that Troy lay under a mound known as Hisarlik, 'the place of the fort'. Hiring an army of 80 workmen, Schliemann set to with typical enthusiasm. He first drove a great trench into the north face of the Hisarlik mound. What he found astonished him, for under the surface lay a jumble of ruins up to 50 ft thick in places. Schliemann was confounded by this mass of evidence and, since modern methods of dating archaeological strata were not then known, he presumed that the ruins were the remains of later cities and that the Troy of legend was surely the bottom layer. With characteristic energy, he plowed downwards for two years, until at last he came to a layer bearing evidence of fire and destruction. At last, he believed, he had found Homer's Troy. Then he made an even more

Right:
Some of the magnificent items excavated by Heinrich Schliemann at the site of Troy, and dubbed by him 'Priam's Treasure', after the city's legendary ruler at the time of the Trojan War. In fact, the treasure predated the Troy of legend by nearly a thousand years. This remarkable collection disappeared from a Berlin museum when the city was taken by the Russians in 1945. Reports following the reunification of Germany in 1990 suggest they may now have been relocated.

Left:
At Mycenae, Schliemann found treasure to rival that of Troy. The golden death masks, one of which Schliemann believed belonged to Agamemnon himself, are well known, but there was much more, including this beautifully wrought gold and cornelian necklace.

Above:
This superb piece of gold jewelry, recovered from Mycenae, dates from about 1500 BC, the date archaeologists give to the Trojan War, if it really did take place. Schliemann's desire to prove the stories of the war as fact laid the foundation for our understanding of the glories of pre-Classical Greece.

dramatic discovery. According to his diary, quite possibly rewritten at a later date, on 14th June 1873 found gold: more than 8,000 golden objects — cups, vases, bracelets, and necklaces. He immediately concluded that this was the hoard of King Priam, Troy's legendary ruler. Schliemann draped his young Greek wife Sophia with some of the more spectacular items — 'The Jewels of Helen' — and had her pose for photographs. To the disgust of the Turkish authorities, he smuggled the jewels out of the country and took them to Berlin.

Troy and Mycenae

It is now accepted by archaeologists that Hisarlik was very likely the site of Troy, and was destroyed no less than nine times during 4,000 years of occupation. It had 47 distinct layers of habitation, from a Neolithic settlement established in 3600 BC to the Roman city of New Ilium, which declined in about AD 500. Schliemann's excavations destroyed many of the later layers, including part of Troy VI, widely held to be Homer's Troy, in his naive drive to find something deeper and older. Schliemann's treasure, in fact, dated from around 2200 BC, nearly 1,000 years before Priam. For all his misdirected enthusiasm, he

had, however, confounded the classical scholars and proved that Troy *did* exist.

What of the gold items themselves? They were housed in the Ethnological Museum in Berlin until the outbreak of World War II, when they were broken up and hidden. Like many other treasures, they have not been seen since the Russians overran the city in 1945.

Fate had more delights in stores for Schliemann. Flushed with his success at Troy, he travelled to Mycenae, another of Homer's heroic kingdoms. In search of the hero Agamemnon, Schliemann dug trenches inside ancient Mycenae's surviving walls and, in spite of classicists' scoffing, made another astonishing find. He uncovered the graves of 19 people — he immediately assumed them to be Agamemnon's family — including those of three men clad in breathtaking gold armor and masks. The story goes that when he removed the mask from the most imposing of the remains, the features on the skull beneath it were still visible. Transfixed, Schliemann, the romantic founding father of archaeology, is said to have cried: 'I have gazed upon the face of Agamemnon!'

'King Solomon's mines'

Above:

The so-called 'acropolis' of Great Zimbabwe. The superb construction of the dry-stone walling, here built to follow the contours and boulders of a natural kopje, convinced racist early explorers that the ruins could not be of African origin. In their search for proof of the mysterious lost race that they imagined had built Zimbabwe. early untrained enthusiasts destroyed most of the evidence of the real Africans who did.

Scattered across modern Zimbabwe and into Mozambique are more than 150 mysterious historic sites, the most famous of which is the ruin Great Zimbabwe, 150 miles east of the city of Bulawayo. Great Zimbabwe comprises no less than 60 acres of imposing ruins, carefully constructed, with formidable dry-stone walls many feet thick and up to 30 ft high. At the center of this complex is the so-called Elliptical Building, a great oval wall, 280 yards in circumference and containing the remains of further stone constructions.

The destruction of African artifacts

For most of the 19th century, the country of Zimbabwe itself was known only through the stories of travellers, hunters, and adventurers, some of whom brought back tales of the dramatic and deserted ruins. To visionary souls in settled South Africa, they suggested evidence of a long-vanished race of ancient splendor. Mixed up with garbled accounts of a fierce native empire nearby — the Matabele — these stories provided the novelist Rider Haggard, for one, with the inspiration for his tale *King*

Solomon's Mines. Zimbabwe was known to contain long-abandoned gold mines, and the promise of mineral wealth prompted empire-builder Cecil Rhodes to float the British South Africa (B.S.A.) Company, which in 1890 occupied Mashonaland, an area that included the Great Zimbabwe ruins.

Colonial attitudes at the time found it hard to accept that native Africans could have constructed such wonders, and the first white settlers followed the prevailing theory that the ruins were the work of some distant superior race — the Phoenicians, perhaps, who held an almost mystical fascination for the Victorians. Rhodes himself was convinced that Great Zimbabwe was the Ophir of the Bible (now claimed by some to have been in Peru). In 1891, the B.S.A. Company, together with the Royal Geographical Society, sponsored an expedition to investigate the origins of the ruins. It was headed by J. Theodore Bent. Bent made extensive digs around the site, to a depth of several feet, but, although he uncovered many African artifacts which he dismissed as 'native rubbish', he could find disappointingly few clues as to the complex's origins. He made a stab at a date — placing construction around 1000 BC — and blandly dismissed the creators as an ancient race from the Middle East.

Evidence of gold workings

Bent, at least, was motivated by a desire for knowledge, but elsewhere in Rhodes' country the lure was naked profit. In 1893, the B.S.A. Company went to war with and defeated the Matabele, and the country was opened up for exploitation by the victors. A noted scout, F. R. Burnham, began to dig in the ruins at Dhlo Dhlo, and was rewarded by a find of 641 oz of gold ornaments. At the Mundie Ruin, two graves were discovered revealing skeletons draped with 208 oz of gold. Evidence of ancient gold workings was plentiful, and it was enthusiastically estimated that they must have produced, in the past, at least 21 million oz of gold. In September 1895, the company gave the Rhodesia Ancient Ruins Ltd Company permission to dig in the historic ruins to search for treasure. Rhodes, who was fascinated by Great Zimbabwe itself, insisted that that site was not to be touched. Nonetheless, the company explored about 50 ruins, turning up another 700 oz of gold at Dhlo Dhlo, and 178 oz from the Chumnungwa and Mtelcgwa sites. Not until several years had elapsed did anyone realize the irretrievable damage that was being done by these haphazard digs.

In May 1902, Richard Hall was appointed curator of the site of Great Zimbabwe. Determined to get to the bottom of the mystery, literally, Hall began excavations to find what he considered to be the level of habitation of the builders of the site. Still looking for the mysterious long-lost race, he ruthlessly cleared out the accumulations of African debris. He found a few gold items, some exotic pottery, and some beads, but of the Phoenicians there was no sign.

What such unenlightened endeavour had done, of course, was to destroy the very evidence it was searching for. In 1929, the first professional archaeologists investigated the ravaged Great Zimbabwe site and concluded that it was probably medieval and undoubtedly African. The 'native rubbish' so carefully purged had been the key to understanding generations of black African habitation. Subsequent work using modern archaeological methods has confirmed that, while the many ruins were built at different times and occupied by changing peoples, all were unquestionably African, and that the citadel of Great Zimbabwe itself was constructed scarcely earlier than 1450. A few handfuls of looted gold were poor compensation for the debunking of a myth, although the spirits of Great Zimbabwe's builders can perhaps take comfort from the fact that Cecil Rhodes' private-enterprise empire is now called Zimbabwe.

Below:
An extraordinary elliptical building lies at the heart of the complex of stone ruins known as Great Zimbabwe. These ruins, rumored to have been built by a long-forgotten, non-African race, fascinated white adventurers who visited them early in the 19th century and were widely believed to conceal gold and gems. Sir Henry Rider Haggard was inspired by such stories to write his bestselling adventure novel King Solomon's Mines *(1885). In the fiction, Haggard's heroes return laden with diamonds. In fact, the ruins' treasures were largely gems of archaeological knowledge.*

Minoan Crete

The legend of Atlantis, the rich island empire suddenly swallowed up by the sea in ancient times, has fascinated scholars and treasure seekers for centuries. The great philosopher Plato (427-347 BC) gave the outline of the story in two of his works and lost Atlantis has been sought across the world ever since. Many regarded it as a myth, like Homer's Troy, but with Schliemann's discoveries at Hisarlik lending substance to the Troy story, a number of amateur archaeologists were spurred to make similar discoveries, and from these have come clues that have led some to believe that Atlantis has at last been found.

Sir Arthur Evans was a British enthusiast who followed in Schliemann's footsteps. He was not inspired by Schliemann's obsession with Troy but, as a scholar, was intrigued by the origins of the Bronze Age civilization that Schliemann had discovered in the Aegean. Evans's interest in early forms of writing, in particular, led him to Crete, where earlier, half-hearted excavations had revealed the existence of extensive ancient ruins. Evans bought a site known as Kephala, a low mound on the coast of northern Crete, long rumored to be the site of a great ruined palace, Knossos, and began excavating in 1899.

The legend of the Minotaur

Evans' finds were no less spectacular that Schliemann's, for he too discovered a previously unknown civilization. Crete was remembered in the old Greek heroic poems as the home of King Minos, a wise and just ruler, cursed with the affliction of a son born half-man, half-bull — the famous Minotaur. Minos demanded tribute from mainland Greece each year, and had human sacrifices given to the Minotaur in the labyrinth (a place so complex that neither the monster nor his victims could find their way out of its maze of corridors). According to the story, the Greek hero Theseus finally slew the Minotaur and escaped by following a thread with which he had carefully plotted his route. Evans took the name from the legend and named his civilization Minoan Crete. Astonishingly, echoes of the Minotaur legend abounded: the Minoans had a clear cult of bull worship, and the remarkably preserved palace at Knossos was indeed constructed with labyrinthine complexity. There were no sensational gold death masks such as Schliemann found at Mycenae, but there were tons of pottery and exquisite bronze figurines, and the palace walls retained frescoes revealing the remarkably vivid and lively cultural and artistic life of the ancient Cretans. And Knossos was not alone — it was merely the dominant city of a civilization that had once covered the whole island of Crete.

The big bang

The question that continues to intrigue scholars interested in Crete is: Why did its Minoan civilization fade away, to be replaced suddenly by Greek cultures from the north? The key lies on the island of Thera (Santorini), 70 miles across the open sea to the north of Crete. Thera today consists of a circle of small islands around a deep bay, the remains of an ancient volcano which once erupted with devastating force. Indeed, there are two small active cones still smoldering in the center of the bay.

Archaeologists estimate that the Minoan civilization collapsed around 1500 BC, only the main complex at Knossos surviving to fall by conquest a generation later. And seismologists know that Thera blew its top in about 1470 BC. The force of the eruption was incredible: thousands of tons of rock and pumice were blown out of the volcano before it collapsed in upon the magma chamber, leaving only the ring of islands and steep cliffs that remain today. Thera's steep cliffs plummet 880 ft to the bay, where the water is so deep that ships cannot anchor. They are carpeted with layers

of volcanic pumice up to 200 ft thick in places. There are no contemporary accounts of the explosion, but there are modern counterparts, such as the earth-shaking eruption of Krakatoa, Java, in 1883. The devastation wrought by Krakatoa was horrific, with up to 300 towns and villages on the Sumatran and Javan mainlands, 50 miles distant, being washed away by tidal waves, and more than 36,380 people losing their lives. Tidal waves reared up to a height of 120 ft above the normal level of the sea and the sun was blotted out by volcanic dust for hundreds of miles. And the evidence suggests that Thera, if anything, was an even larger explosion than Krakatoa.

Could an eruption on Thera have been responsible for the overnight collapse of the Minoans? Certainly, the bulk of the Minoan palaces were on the exposed northern coasts of Crete. In 1966, south of Akrotiri village on Thera itself, archaeologists discovered a fine Minoan colony, competely buried in volcanic pumice. Some of the palaces on Crete reveal ample evidence of volcanic fallout, and they were fatally exposed to the risk of tidal waves. Only Knossos, the one palace to survive, was situated on high ground a safe distance from the sea. And, in the image of a great island culture suddenly swallowed up in one night of earthquake, fire, and flood, surely we find all the staple ingredients of the later Greek story — 'Lost Atlantis'.

Below left:
The civilization of the Minoan Cretans predated that of Classical Greece, and possessed a remarkably exuberant artistic and cultural life. The lively murals discovered and restored by Evans at the palace at Knossos, one of the very few Minoan centers to escape the sudden and mysterious destruction, are a true artistic treasure.

Below:
A huge storage jar from the palace at Knossos. Many such jars have been found at other Minoan sites, often cracked or broken by the heat of a smothering layer of volcanic tephra, evidence of the cataclysmic eruption that is thought to have destroyed the Minoan civilization.

Lost Cities of the Incas

Above:

The conquistadores of the 16th century saw value only in the bullion and precious stones of the Indian cultures they plundered, but today untold damage is done to historic sites by thieves who hack out stone carvings, highly prized on the black market for their artistic and cultural value. This elaborately incised stele from 1000 BC gives a good impression of what attracts the modern plunderers who follow in Pizarro's footsteps.

When the conquistador Francisco Pizarro entered the empire of the Inca in September 1532, he had with him a tiny army of just 130 footsoldiers and 40 horsemen. Yet within a few years he was to devastate Inca lands and plunder one of the greatest treasure houses in history. For, although they were a highly disciplined people with a strong army, the Inca empire completely underestimated the ruthlessness and thorough brutality of the invaders. When the Inca himself, Atahualpa, Emperor and Child of the Sun God, visited Pizarro in November 1532, the Spaniards launched an unprovoked attack which slaughtered many of his followers and made Atahualpa himself prisoner. When Atahualpa noticed, contemptuously, that all the conquistadores seemed to want was gold, he offered to fill a room 22 ft long by 17 ft wide to a height of 8 ft with gold, and twice more with silver, in return for his freedom.

For six months Inca messengers scoured the country, collecting their nation's wealth, most of it beautifully worked offerings to the gods. But Pizarro had no fine feelings toward art and, in one of the greatest acts of vandalism of all time, had the whole lot melted down. It produced some 11 tons of gold and 25,000 lb of silver, a breathtaking haul by contemporary standards, and estimated to be worth over $2000 million at today's prices. Atahualpa fulfilled his promise, but Pizarro broke his, and had Atahualpa killed anyway. He then marched on Cuzco, the Inca capital. Brushing aside all opposition, he occupied the city and began systematically looting temples and treasure houses. From Cuzco alone he took items reduced to 2.5 tons of gold and 51.5 tons of silver. Pizarro installed a puppet ruler, Manco, in Atahualpa's place, and for two years the invaders methodically stripped the Inca lands of their remaining riches.

Manco defies the Spaniards

But the Spanish outrages grew too much even for Manco, and in May 1536 he led a revolt that trapped the Spaniards in Cuzco and came within an ace of destroying them. Pizarro, however, managed to rally his forces, counterattacked, and held out until reinforcements arrived. Manco was forced onto the defensive and began to retreat into the mountains northwest of Cuzco, building a new capital at Vitcos. When a Spanish punitive expedition located it, he abandoned it, and established himself at Vilcabamba. This was an area so remote, cut off by mountain ranges and rainforest, that he was able to use it as a safe base from which to wage a guerrilla war for several years. Not until June 1572, when Manco himself was dead and Spanish rule throughout the rest of Inca lands was established, did a column finally reach and occupy Vilcabamba. The last of the Inca's subjects, retreating before the Spaniards, carried away what remained of the city's wealth and fired the buildings.

Search for the lost city

For centuries, as the jungle reclaimed Manco's last refuges, the legend of the 'lost city of the Incas' fired the imagination of travellers. In the early 19th century, several expeditions explored remote Inca ruins. In 1850, a Frenchman named Angrand openly admitted, while tearing holes in a site later identified as Choquequirau, that he was lured by rumors of 'immense treasure...buried among the ruins when the survivors of the race of the sun retired to the savage asylum'. Needless to say, he didn't find any.

A young American archaeologist, Hiram Bingham, whose motives were somewhat purer, was rewarded in 1911 by the discovery of an overgrown city perched on a mountain top 2,000 ft above the Urubamba River, west of Cuzco. When the layers of jungle growth were cleared, it was found that the buildings and terraces were in a remarkable state of preservation.

Bingham was convinced that his site, called by the locals Machu Picchu, was the legendary lost Vilcabamba, and his identification was accepted, with some reservation, until an expedition in 1964 found a further complex hidden two days' journey farther along the Urubamba. This site is now widely believed to be the real Vilcabamba, although its inaccessibility has defied even modern archaeological methods. What is more, although it is an undoubted treasure, historically speaking, it is extremely unlikely that its fleeing inhabitants, already impoverished and on the run, or the pursuing conquistadores, left behind anything of financial value.

Top far left:
The mighty Inca fortress of Sucsayhuaman. From here, in 1536, Manco Inca Yupanqui launched his revolt on the Spaniards in nearby Cuzco. He was nearly successful, but the conquistadores rallied, and Manco was forced to retreat further and further into the impenetrable Andes. He built a number of mountain refuges, the last of which, Vilcabamba, the 'Lost City of the Incas', has still to be properly explored. Although stories of forgotten treasures persist, it is unlikely that Manco's hard-pressed and impoverished followers left anything valuable behind.

Left:
A beautiful gold mask from Peru; very little such work survives, because the conquistadores melted down Atahualpa's ransom, and whatever else they looted, for its bullion.

Below:
A beautiful Chimu ornament from the Peruvian coast. Of no interest whatever to the philistine Spaniards, such pieces are highly valued today.

The search for El Dorado

America and along the Andean cordillera in the hope of finding further gold-rich peoples to plunder. These first expeditions were drawn by tales of rich tribes who always seemed to live beyond the next mountain range, but it was not until the 1540s that these stories began to crystallize into the legend of El Dorado, the fabulous 'Golden Man'.

The legend grows

Somewhere in the mountains around present-day Bogotá, in Colombia, it was said, lived a tribe who made daily offerings to the Sun God. Each morning, before dawn, the chief of the tribe would anoint his body with oil and resin, and his attendants would cover him in finely powered gold dust, which would stick to him until his whole body, from the top of his head to the soles of his feet, glowed with this radiant second skin. With his attendants, and watched by crowds of his people from the shore, the chief would sail out into the middle of a lake. As the first rays of the sun struck him, the chief would dive into the water and, while his attendants threw gold items in after him as offerings, wash himself clean. The legend of a land so rich that it could afford such extravagant daily rituals, together with the image of a lake full of priceless treasures waiting to be recovered, came to obsess the Spanish captains in the New World. And the story grew with the telling. El Dorado became a place, not a man, where all the inhabitants wore nothing but powdered gold, and which boasted not one but two cities whose buildings were made entirely of gold.

Rival expeditions set out across the Andes, some heading northeastward, through Colombia to Venezuela, others descending into the great basin of the Amazon. A few did manage to locate wealthy tribes and returned successful, but many, ranging across bleak highland plateaus, through swamps and impenetrable rainforests, found only hostile Indians, privation, madness, and violent death. The rest discovered nothing but disillusion. Even the great British adventurer Sir Walter Raleigh made two expeditions. One, in 1595, explored reaches of the Orinoco; the other, in 1617, proved an embarrassing failure and indirectly cost Sir Walter his head.

Above:
El Dorado was not the 'golden city' of popular imagination, but in fact a fabulous 'Golden Man'. That the Colombian Indians followed a gold-man cult seems undeniable, as this superb mask and headdress bear witness, but the search for the source of the story, with its untold riches, has lured many to death and disappointment across the ages.

The search for the legendary riches of El Dorado must rank as one of the most famous treasure hunts of all time. In 20 years, beginning with Hernán Cortés' expedition to Mexico in 1519, small bands of Spanish adventurers, the tough and ruthless conquistadores, laid waste to the huge native empires of the New World — those of the Aztecs and the Incas. The riches won from such sorties staggered even those greedy soldiers-of-fortune and, from the 1530s, expeditions began roving through Central

Left:
Lake Guatavita in Colombia, the extraordinary natural phenomenon at the heart of the El Dorado legend. Many attempts have been made to drain the brooding and mysterious lake, none of them successful, although a number of treasures have been uncovered. It remains to be seen whether modern methods, under the watchful eye of trained archaeologists, can fathom the lake's mysteries — or indeed, whether it has any secrets left to give up.

Far right:
The most popular version of the El Dorado legend has it that the Muisca Indians (in what is now Colombia) used to make sacrifices to the Sun God by tossing priceless treasures from a raft into the depths of a lake. The discovery of items such as this gold Muisca piece depicting a raft has not only lent credence to the story, but also given a tantalizing taste of the treasures themselves.

Below:
This gold 'Sun God' mask is from Ecuador. It is easy to see how such objects fired the imagination of those searching for El Dorado.

Focus on Lake Guatavita

And yet the legend lived on. As early as 1560, the lake in the El Dorado legend was being specifically identified as Lake Guatavita, a flooded volcanic crater northeast of Bogotá. Certainly there was some circumstantial evidence to support this. The local people, the Muisca (Chibcha), were wealthy in gold when the conquistadores arrived, and did sometimes make offerings to deities thought to inhabit lakes. The first attempt to recover gold from Lake Guatavita occurred in 1562 when Antonio de Sepulveda dug a trench which drained a few feet of water from the lake; he was rewarded with '232 pesos and 10 grams of good gold'. Other attempts were made, but it was not until the 1820s that anything came of them. An enthusiast name José Ignacio 'Pepe' Paris, aided by an English naval captain, Charles Stuart Cochrane, dug several trenches and tunnels which drained considerable quantities of water from the lake, but produced no gold. Nothing daunted, devotees estimated that the wealth hidden in Lake Guatavita must have been worth $300 million and when, in 1856, a small but beautifully wrought gold Muisca figure, depicting a chief and attendants on a ceremonial raft, was found at nearby Lake Siecha, it seemed that the El Dorado legend was confirmed.

In 1900, an English company, Contractors Limited, succeeded in draining much of the lake, although they were defeated by sludge in the deep center and by the fact that the sun soon baked exposed silt to concrete. Nonetheless they retrieved a number of gold items which were later auctioned at Sothebys in London. In 1932, an American marine diver, Jonesson, found a gold fish, death masks, ritual vessels, pins, and pendants at the water's edge. As recently as 1965 an attempt was made to explore the lake's depths using modern diving equipment, but it was frustrated by the Colombian authorities, who were unwilling to see further amateur exploitation of an archaeological site. And so Lake Guatavita still holds a fascination for those fired by the imaged riches of its depths — despite the fact that the El Dorado legend itself has long since been discredited.

The Lost Dutchman mine

Lost mines, their location bequeathed as treasure maps by dying prospectors, are the very stuff of treasure tales, and the story of the Lost Dutchman mine has all the added ingredients of a good Western — bloodthirsty Indians, gold lust, greed, and murder. And like a lot of classic treasure legends, the facts are so cocooned in half-truth and myth that it is no longer possible to sift reality from rumor.

The story of the Lost Dutchman mine began, like so many concerning gold in the Americas, with a conquistador, Antonio de Espeja, a mining engineer who wandered north through Mexico and discovered silver ore in Arizona in 1582. It is generally accepted that Jesuit miners were the first to exploit this, as they had done elsewhere, until hostile Apaches massacred them.

Gold east of Phoenix

In the mid-1800s, the family of one Enrico Peralta discovered gold somewhere in the Superstition Mountains, some 40 miles east of Phoenix. They exploited it for several years, until they too fell foul of the local Apaches. One day in 1864, the Indians ambushed the Peraltas' gold convoy, and after a fierce three-day battle, wiped it out. A few years later, a surviving member of the Peralta family, Don Miguel, was rescued from a brawl in Sonora by two emigrant Germans, Jacob Waltz and Jacob Weiser. Impressed by their resourcefulness, Don Miguel told them the story of the mine, and offered them a share if they would accompany him into Apache country to retrieve some of the cached gold. They agreed to this, and in 1871 returned from a successful expedition some $60,000 the richer. Peralta took a 50 percent share and presumably retired in comfort. With 25 percent each, Waltz and Weiser gradually ran out of money, and in 1879 made a return journey. They apparently found two Mexicans working the site and had no qualms about shooting them. One day while Waltz was away from the camp, Weiser disappeared. Apache arrows and bloodstained clothing were evidence of his fate. Waltz left the mountains as fast as he could, but in fact Weiser survived in the Indians' attack and was treated by a doctor for his wounds. To this doctor he apparently told the story of the mine before he died.

Waltz, meanwhile, moved to Phoenix. In 1880 two young ex-soldiers rode into the town of Pinal one day with saddlebags full of gold. Questioned as to where they found it, they said they had stumbled on a mine by accident. It was assumed that the men had found the Lost Dutchman — archaically named for Waltz's foreign ancestry. The news soon spread and the two men offered to return to the mine.

Several days later they were found dead. They had been stripped naked in the Apache fashion, but had been shot with a US Army revolver. Suspicion fell on several locals, and the odd eyebrow was raised at Waltz, but nothing was proved.

A deathbed confession

In 1890, Waltz himself went back to find some gold he had hidden with Weiser. He returned with about $1,500 worth. It was his last haul, for he died a year later. On his deathbed he not only confessed to the murder of a nephew, Julius, to whom he'd told the story and then regretted it, but also described the whereabouts of the mine. Funnel-shaped, the mine was in a canyon not far from Weaver's Needle, a prominent local landmark. At least two of those who heard Waltz's last words, Dick Holmes and Reinhart Petrash, tried to locate it, but without success.

A number of indications that mining activity once took place near Weaver's Needle have been discovered, but while the mine continues to attract treasure seekers, it has not been found. Waltz himself may have attempted to disguise the site. Another story relates that the Apaches obliterated all trace of it before they were driven out of the mountains in 1885. But strange things continue to happen in the Superstition Mountains. In 1928, two deer hunters reported that someone had tried to roll rocks down on them. In 1931, 66-year-old Adolph Ruth set off with what he hoped was a copy of Peralta's map. He was found dead, shot through the temple, months later, the map stolen. In 1932, two hikers were shot at by an unknown sniper. As late as 1959, a treasure hunter named Stanley Fernandez was murdered by his partner, Benjamin Ferreira, after they quareled about sharing the workload involved in discovering the mine.

Above:
As the great American West was opened up in the 19th century, prospectors searched for riches in its mountains and along its rivers. For most, rewards were elusive.

Right:
Mysterious, harsh, inhospitable, the Superstition Mountains of Arizona are the site of perhaps the greatest 'lost mine' mystery. The story of the Lost Dutchman mine is a true tale with all the ingredients of a good Western — gold, greed, marauding Indians, and murder. A fortune awaits anyone who dares to defy the ominous and frequently fatal precedents associated with the mine.

4

Grave Goods and Religious Treasures

Treasures associated with religion can be conveniently classified into two main categories: artifacts interred with the dead, and artifacts which may have little or no intrinsic value, but which are thought of as priceless by members of a particular faith.

The practice of burying people of rank together with their most treasured possessions was a remarkably widespread one in ancient times. People as widely separated from each other by culture and the centuries as the Egyptians, the Celts, the Chinese, and the American Indians all buried their important dead with valued grave goods. In each case, the theory was largely the same: the prince, emperor, or chieftain was allowed everything which might make his situation as comfortable in the afterlife as it had been in the present one. And this often included the provision of slaves, servants, and wives, such unfortunates being sacrificed to accompany their master on his spiritual journey.

But not everyone respected the sanctity of such arrangements, even during the deceased's own times. It has been said that the first grave

robbery took place a few hours after the first rich funeral, and certainly down the ages there have been fierce struggles between those who attempted to ensure that a rich grave remained intact and those who wished to plunder it. Whatever the culture, whenever the period, few rich tombs across the world have escaped the attention of despoilers.

Pillage in Egypt

The pillaged tombs of the Egyptian pharaohs are perhaps the best known. With their highly developed cult of the dead, it was essential that orthodox believers be buried with appropriate ceremony for the afterlife. We know from the tomb of Tutankhamum what extraordinary riches went into the grave with a dead prince or king. Superb jewels, figurines, magnificent coffins — gold, gold, and yet more gold. But Tutankhamun's tomb achieved its fame precisely because it was intact — it was the only one of all the graves in the Valley of the Kings to have been overlooked by grave-robbers. How tempting it must have been for ordinary Egyptians, knowing of such burials, to risk divine displeasure and severe punishment

if caught for the chance of instant wealth in the here and now!

Despite the efforts of zealous priests, grave-robbing was often systematically and cynically organized by the very officials who were supposed to prevent it. It is known that many officials connived at the robbery of bodies before the tombs were sealed. Coffins have been found with built-in devices to aid robbers — disguised wooden panels which could easily be tapped out to facilitate the rifling of the body. The mummies themselves, which often had valuable charms wrapped into their bandages, were frequently simply stolen. As recently as 1985, the grave of Nephrenbet, a chief minister of Rameses II, was discovered. His sarcophagus, made of rose-colored granite, is one of the largest yet found, but when workmen removed the 7-ton lid they found that thieves had drilled a hole in the bottom and stolen the contents.

All the ingenious booby traps, false passages, and other disguises built into many tombs were of no avail. It is curious, however, that few rulers seem to have resorted to the one means of protecting the dead which continues to grip 20th-century imaginations: the curse. Most Egyptian tombs simply bear inscriptions begging intruders to pray for the soul of the departed.

An exception is the tomb of Yaba, queen of the bloodthirsty Assyrians in the 8th century BC, discovered at Nimrud, northern Iraq, in 1988. There, a stone table carried the dire warning 'Whoever in future...removes me from my resting place, casts evil designs on my jewelry, or opens this grave, his ghost will wander thirsting in the sun forever.' Iraqi archaeologists braved the malediction to unearth a stupendous cache of exquisite golden artifacts, including 90 necklaces, 80 earrings, and a diadem. The work was halted in 1991 by the Gulf War, as though in terrible fulfilment of Queen Yaba's curse.

Early excavators

Until the birth of real archaeology in the 19th century, inquisitive individuals investigating ancient tombs were little more than grave-robbers themselves. It was not until well into this century that proper techniques for understanding strata, the layers of soil in which items are buried, were developed. Most early investigators simply saw their job as being to recover whatever valuables might have been left at a particular site. They lacked the facilities to understand much else.

The first attempts to dig into the Roman

Above:
Tombs in the necropolis of the Etruscan town of Caeri (modern Cerveteri) in northern Italy. Etruscan tombs have been preyed on by plunderers ever since they were built.

Above left:
A 13th-century AD stone pipe unearthed from an American Indian burial site in Oklahoma. The two carved figures probably represent a ritual sacrifice.

cities of Herculaneum and Pompeii in the 18th century were naked treasure hunts, marked by organized gangs looting valuable statues wholesale, although later attempts were made to record what was uncovered. When, in 1776, the Duke of Northumberland dug a shaft into Silbury Hill in England, his prime aim was to discover a life-sized gold equestrian statue he believed was buried there. By the end of the century, it was realized that much could be learned from such sites, but excavators were still primarily interested in removing items of value — albeit historic value, rather than strictly intrinsic.

A few of the early excavators did apply more restrained standards. No less a person than Thomas Jefferson was one of the first to be interested by evidence of old American Indian cultures. In 1784, he opened up a burial mound in Virginia. He was not looking for valuable grave goods, but simply trying to learn. With a thoroughness worthy of a modern archaeologist, he noted that the mound was clearly a tomb, for it contained a large number of skeletons, buried in layers at apparently different times. By studying the remains, he came to the conclusion that the site was a civilian cemetery, not a mass war grave as had previously been supposed, because several of the skeletons were those of women and children and none bore marks of weapons.

Historic treasures

Some sites do, occasionally, survive the ravages of despoilers and the modern world is allowed a breathtaking insight into the glories of years gone by. We have already mentioned Tutankhamun; the tombs of some of the Chinese emperors have also revealed quite stunning jade burial suits and artifacts. And the life-size terracotta army of Ch'in Shih Huang-Ti, far too cumbersome and valueless to tempt robbers, has been revealed to amaze us today. A 6th-century BC Celtic grave at Vix, in France, escaped the attention of thieves and was found to contain the tomb of a wealthy and influential woman, accompanied by her brooches, rings, armlets, a diadem of gold, a bronze statuette, and a huge bronze vessel from Greece. The least valuable of the items intrinsically, the bronze statuette, turned out to be the most interesting, because it proved the existence of hitherto unsuspected trade routes.

The practice of stripping ancient tombs is not, alas, over. Many valuable sites remain hidden to professional archaeologists, who often lack the resources to explore fully those sites they do know of. With high prices paid on the international market for examples of ancient art, the unscrupulous and cunning find ready outlets. The sites of ancient Etruscan tombs in Italy, and Anatolian ones in Turkey, are widely rumored to be plundered by professionals who keep the locations to themselves. Even communist China found it helpful to employ the expertise of known tomb-robbers when trying to excavate imperial tombs in the 1960s. It is quite impossible to guess at the nature and value of the goods which have disappeared, over the centuries, from graves around the world.

Sacred treasure

Among the most revered of holy relics are alleged fragments of the cross on which Jesus of Nazareth was crucified (although it must be

Below:
One of the treasures of Ur, a golden bull's head, decorated with lapis lazuli, adorns a lyre. Objects surviving from ancient graves represent only a fraction of the original treasure, a tantalizing glimpse of what has been lost down the ages.

said that if all the portions were gathered together in one place they would make up not one but several 'true' crosses of the correct dimensions). Relics of the saints, including clothing, possessions, and even parts of their bodies, have also been lovingly hoarded in shrines and churches around the world for centuries.

Probably the most famous of all is the Turin Shroud, an ancient cloth bearing bloodstains and the image of a man with a bearded face. For centuries, it was claimed to be the winding sheet in which Jesus's body was wrapped after the Crucifixion, and as such was reverently guarded in Turin Cathedral. When, in 1988, the church authorities finally allowed scientific tests to be carried out on the shroud, it was found with near-certainty, to date from around AD 1300. But although it now seems to be an elaborate fake, the technique used to create the image still puzzles art experts.

2,000-year-old scrolls

A multiple holy treasure, discovered as recently as 1947, was unearthed by a young Arab boy chasing a stray goat near the Dead Sea, the lake that lies between Israel and Jordan. In a cave he found cylinders containing 11 scrolls. The boy and a friend sold their find to a Jerusalem dealer for a few dollars. Long afterwards, the Syrian Orthodox Monastery of St Mark paid well over $100,000 for five of the manuscripts, now known as the Dead Sea Scrolls.

The scrolls are written in Hebrew and Aramaic, and experts have dated them to between 100 BC and AD 68 (before this epic find, the oldest biblical books in Hebrew were about half that age). Together they represent some 500 books, about 100 of which are versions of the Old Testament books of the Bible. They also describe the life and times of the community that lived in and around a monastery known as Khirbet Qumran.

Below:
Most graves thought to contain valuables have been plundered in past centuries, but occasionally one is found intact, and contains such a wealth of dazzling treasures that it becomes legendary. The tomb of Tutankhamun made even experienced archaeologist Howard Carter feel the excited anticipation of a treasure seeker when he first peered into it. This gold statue was among the many stupendous artifacts in the pharoah's tomb.

Left:
Inside the 'Palace of Virgins', a mound grave from the Macedonian empire of 250-300 BC, visitors can see a stone copy of the original wooden throne.

The treasures of the Chinese emperors

Like the pharaohs of Egypt, the emperors of China went to their graves accompanied by a magnificent panoply to serve them well in the afterlife. And, just like the pharaohs, they were haunted by the thought that their last resting places were highly likely to be desecrated by grave-robbers. The practice of grave-robbing is as universal, and virtually as old, as the practice of burying valuables with their deceased owners. The battle between those who built tombs, and tried to ensure their protection, and those who defiled them, stretches across time to the mists of antiquity.

In China, it was the habit of emperors to build tombs as virtual underground palaces, covering them with a large burial mound, often acres in extent, and surrounded by a protecting wall. Sometimes the resulting hill was planted with trees in a naive attempt to pass it off as a natural formation. Apparent entrances were often false and, as the tomb-builders increased their skill through experience, interior passages frequently included booby traps. It was all to no avail, for the vast majority of imperial tombs in China were entered and plundered centuries ago. So expert were the tomb-robbers that when an archaeological expedition sought to excavate the tomb of the Emperor Ming Wan Li near Peking in the 1960s, known professional tomb-robbers were released from prison on parole as 'special archaeological assistants'. Sure enough, they located the hidden entrance to the tomb with ease.

Tempting relics

The discovery of tombs which have survived desecration indicates that extraordinary riches could reward enterprising thieves. In 1968, a unit of the People's Liberation Army was carrying out construction work near Man-Ch'eng when they came across an artificial cave in a hillside. Archaeologists found two vast underground chambers — one 170 ft long by 121 ft wide — which proved to be the graves of Prince Liu Sheng, a member of the royal family during the Western Han Dynasty, who died in 113 BC, and his wife Dou Wan. The graves had not been plundered, and foremost among the treasures discovered were the jade suits in which the bodies had been buried. Taoist magicians believed that jade had the property of preventing the decay of a body after death. In this case it was ineffectual, as only a few bones remained and the suits had collapsed, but upon restoration these proved to be quite stunning. Liu Sheng's suit was some 74 inches long and made up of 2,498 wafers of jade held together by 2½ lb of gold thread. His wife's was 67¾ inches long, with 2,160 pieces

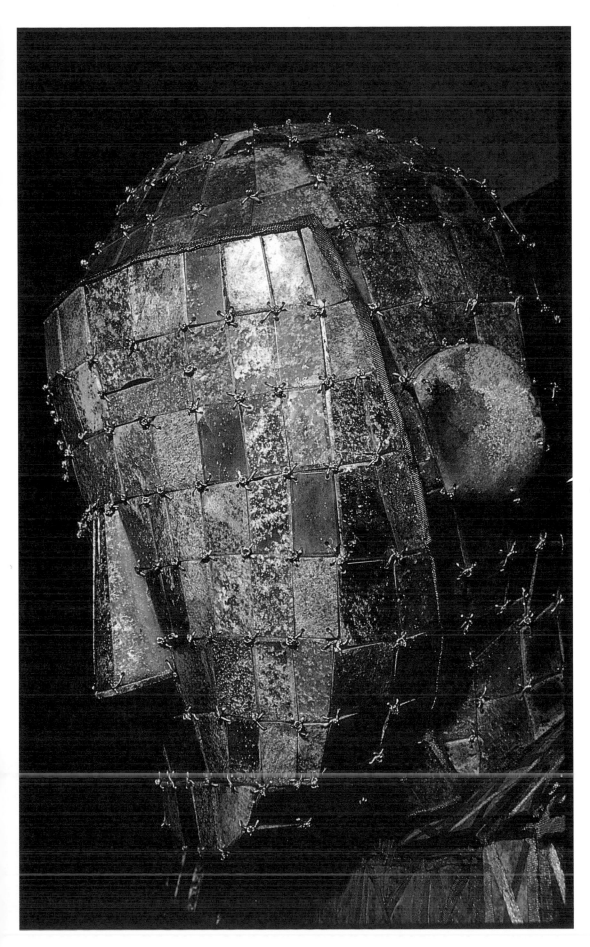

Far left:
Row upon row of terracotta infantrymen form part of the life-size army of 1,000 warriors set to guard the tomb of the Chinese Emperor Ch'in Shih Huang-Ti, China's 'First Emperor' (221–210 BC) and builder of the Great Wall. The Mount Lishan mound is one of the most extraordinary archaeological sites in the world.

Left:
According to Taoist beliefs, jade prevented decay of a body after death. In the case of Prince Liu Sheng and his wife Dou Wan, this proved to be a myth, for when archaeologists opened their tomb at Man Ch'eng they found few human remains, but the suits themselves are of incredible beauty and priceless value. This is the face mask and head covering of the Princess.

of jade and 1¹/₄ lb of gold. Over 2,000 priceless bronze, pottery, and jade items were also found.

At least one grave-robber was caught in the act and his fate left for all to see. According to legend, the young Princess Yung T'ai fell foul of her grandmother, the fearsome Empress Wu, who had both the princess and her husband put to death in about AD 701. After the empress' death, the couple were re-interred by a grieving relative in a burial mound 37 ft high near Ch'ien-hsien. In 1964, when the tomb was excavated, archaeologists found a skeleton near the mouth of a tunnel dug by thieves; a trail of valuables, dropped in haste, led back to the graves.

Recent discoveries

Perhaps the most remarkable tomb ever discovered was that of Ch'in Shih Huang-Ti, the 'First Emperor', a fierce autocrat who in the 3rd century BC united China by conquering warring tribes. He is best remembered as the builder of the famous Great Wall. He was buried beneath a mound 164 ft high, Mount Lishan, in the valley of the Yellow River. Despite protective devices, such as crossbows set to be triggered by the movements of an intruder, it was widely known that the tomb had been rifled. In March 1974, however, peasants digging a well a mile or so from the site uncovered some terracotta figures, which proved to be part of an army of literally thousands of life-size figures. Archaeologists patiently clearing the site believe it will be years before their work is completed, but now hope that Ch'in Shih Huang-Ti may have left his burial mound as a decoy and that his real resting place may yet be undisturbed. If so, a treasure of legendary proportions may await the finders, for the First Emperor went to the afterlife surrounded by entire rivers made of mercury and accompanied by a map made of precious metals.

Finds continue to be made. In 1983, the hill of Xianggan, north of Canton, was leveled, unearthing the tomb of the Emperor Wen Di. He was dressed in the traditional jade burial suit and had been accompanied to the grave by six servants, one a woman still cradling the skeleton of a child, four concubines, and dozens of jade, silver, ivory, agate, and glass artifacts, including 43 jade ritual swords carved with dragons and tigers.

One tomb which continues to elude the searchers, however, is that of the first Ming emperor, who ruled from AD 1369. The graves of 13 Ming emperors are known to exist near Peking, but the first took extraordinary measures to prevent discovery. He had no less than 13 coffins prepared for 13 tombs, and nobody knew which contained the body and its treasures when all 13 were buried with appropriate pomp and ceremony. In 1928, roadmakers uncovered a promising tunnel near Nanking, but it proved to be a false lead, and the real grave and its treasures have not yet been found despite diligent research.

Right:
Enigmatic smiles distinguish the features in this delicate portrait of these court ladies from the Tang dynasty. The smiles hint at many mysteries about the tombs of the ancient emperors, some of which have still to be found, and which may, if the grave robbers have not ruined them, contain fabulous wealth.

Tutankhamun

'Can you see anything?' 'Yes — wonderful things!' With this, surely one of the most famous exchanges in archaeological history, Egyptologist Howard Carter and his patron, Lord Carnarvon, peered through a hole they had made in the sealed entrance and became the first living persons in 33 centuries to gaze upon the tomb of the pharaoh Tutankhamun.

Carter's discovery of the tomb was scarcely an accident, although he certainly had more than his fair share of luck. He had begun searching the Valley of the Kings, a desolate valley near Thebes in Egypt (where no less than 49 ancient rulers were buried), in 1914, financed by his wealthy English backer, Lord Carnarvon. Many archaeologists thought that the site was exhausted. Although Carter found several clues which led him to believe that Tutankhamun's tomb was in the valley, he had had no luck in finding it. By 1922, Carnarvon's money was beginning to run out and only one small section of the valley remained to be explored. This was a small triangle of rock and sand at the foot of the already discovered tomb of Rameses IV.

The great discovery

Determined to have one last try, Carter ordered this patch of ground to be cleared. As he went on site on the morning of 4th November, Carter was greeted by silence from his normally noisy workmen; they had uncovered a flight of steps leading down into the ground. Hurriedly, Carter cleared the rubble and found that the steps led to a door bearing seals in the name of Tutankhamun. With remarkable restraint, Carter cabled Lord Carnarvon, at home in England, and waited for him to arrive. Not until 25th November was the door opened. It revealed a long passage leading to another door. Here Carter made a small hole in the upper left-hand corner, held up a candle to test for escaping gases, and peered in.

Tutankhamun himself was not a particularly significant figure. He reigned from 1361 to 1352 BC, and died at the age of 18, probably violently. His only real historical importance was that he succeeded Akhenaton, a heretic pharaoh who had broken with traditional Egyptian beliefs and founded his

Left:
The sun-baked Valley of the Kings, where Howard Carter searched for years for Tutankhamun's tomb. He finally found it tucked in a hidden corner, overshadowed by the graves of mightier kings — but, unlike any of the others in the valley, Tutankhamun's had escaped the attentions of ancient grave-robbers.

Far left:
The step pyramid of Saqqara is older than the better known pyramids at Gizeh, near Cairo. The pharaohs went to great lengths to protect the treasures buried in their tombs, but the conspicuous pyramids soon attracted the attention of grave-robbers, and few tombs escaped plundering. The boy-king Tutankhamun's did so precisely because it looked so insignificant from above ground.

own religion. During the reign of the young and pliant Tutankhamun, the religious establishment had reasserted its power and restored the old gods. After his death, Tutankhamun was quickly forgotten. And this, ironically, was what ensured his immortality and made the discovery of his tomb so important. For, alone among all the long-dead inhabitants of the Valley of the Kings, Tutankhamun's tomb had been left largely undisturbed by grave-robbers, who had systematically plundered all the other sites, sometimes within hours of the burial. What Carter saw when his eyes became accustomed to the gloom was the full panoply of an Ancient Egyptian royal burial.

Above:
Tutankhamun's throne is considered by many to be the supreme artistic treasure of his tomb. A beautifully worked and inlaid gold panel depicts the king sitting at ease, while his queen anoints his shoulder. The treasures of Tutankhamun's tomb are without parallel in the field of Egyptology.

Far right:
Uncanny in its beauty and priceless in value, this is Tutankhamun's death mask, a lifelike effigy in gold, inlaid with obsidian and lapis lazuli, which rested on the shoulders of the body itself. Carter believed that it captured perfectly the tranquil expression of the young king overtaken prematurely by death.

Priceless relics

The tomb itself consisted of four rooms: a large antechamber, a small annex, the sealed-off coffin room itself, and an attendant treasure room. With typical patience, Carter set to work cataloging, restoring, and removing the contents of each room before moving on to the next. The bone-dry conditions within the tomb had ensured that even fragile, organic materials such as wood and basketwork survived the ages. In the antechamber alone there were large wooden gilded couches, life-size statues, a golden throne, and a jumble of vases, shrines, and boxes containing items for the king's comfort in the afterlife. Carter processed them all before moving on to the sepulchre. Watched by an audience of mesmerized officials, Carter broke into the burial chamber itself on 17th February 1923. He was greeted by a wall of gold, the outer casing of a gilded casket so large that it almost filled the chamber. Tutankhamun's coffin proved a veritable Chinese box; inside the outer shrine lay another, and another, and another, and inside that a shaped granite sarcophagus. Within this

lay three coffins, the first made of gilded wood, the second of wood covered with gold leaf, and the third, breathtakingly beautiful, of solid gold inlaid with precious stones and jewels. Nor was that all. When he carefully peeled away the layers of petrified funeral ointments, Carter found that the mummy itself wore a stunning gold death mask.

It took Carter five years to preserve and remove the treasures of the tomb — statues, figurines, pieces of chariots, jewels, weapons — to the Cairo Museum, and a further five to finish cataloging them. Their value was inexpressible — the inner coffin alone weighed 300 lb, worth perhaps $250,000 just in bullion value. Yet Lord Carnarvon, whose money had made the discovery possible, did not live long to appreciate it. He died six months after the find from an infected mosquito bite, giving rise to the legend of the Pharaoh's Curse, an idea which still grips the popular imagination, despite the fact that the hieroglyphics on Tutankhamun's tomb make no mention of a curse and the fact that Carter himself lived to the age of 64.

The Sutton Hoo burial

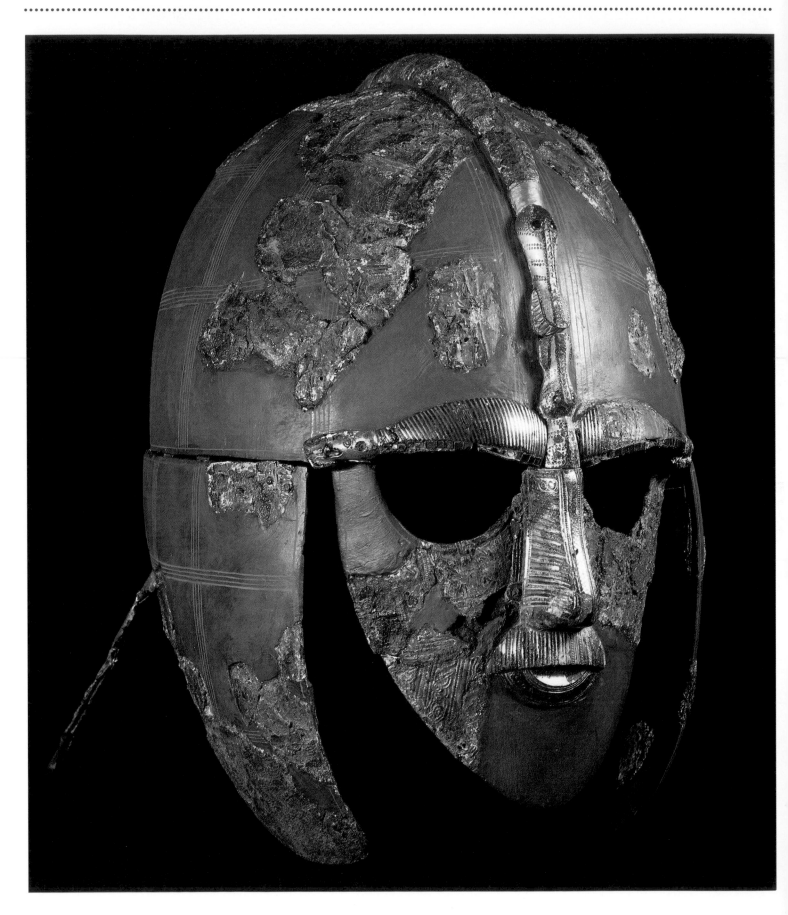

The Sutton Hoo burial

At Sutton Hoo, near the village of Woodbridge in Suffolk, England, there is a cluster of 15 or more grassed-over ancient burial mounds, or barrows. Unlike many of the important archaeological sites of the Mediterranean, the Middle East, or the Americas, there was no great mystery about the Sutton Hoo site; its location was widely known and its purpose easily guessed. It was not until the 1930s, however, that any attempt was made to excavate the site, an enterprise rewarded by the discovery of one of the richest treasures in British archaeological history.

In 1938, the local magistrate, who owned the land on which the barrows were situated, gave permission for an amateur enthusiast to make some exploratory diggings. Several of the sites were opened and it was confirmed that they were burial mounds dating from the Dark Ages between the collapse of the Roman occupation and the Norman Conquest in 1066. One even contained traces of a wooden boat, suggesting that it might have been a ship-burial of a type associated with the Vikings. All the barrows had been disturbed many years before by treasure seekers, however, and were badly damaged; the ship site, in particular, had been almost obliterated.

A ship-burial mound

The next season, in 1939, the same team turned their attention to the largest of the mounds, some 9 ft high, without any great hopes of success. As they cut into the sandy soil, however, they came across a line of iron bolts — rivets from the planking of an ancient ship, still in their correct positions and therefore apparently undisturbed. Evidence of another ship-burial emerged and, when the team reached the center of the ship, where the body and funeral goods would have been laid to rest, they found enough items to convince them that it had escaped plundering. Since the site was clearly of the greatest importance, a team of professionals from the British Museum was called in and a full-scale excavation got under way.

The results were astonishing. When the barrow was fully excavated, it was found that it had indeed covered a wooden ship some 89 ft long. The timbers had long since rotted away, but they had left a curiously precise impression in the soil where they had been, and all the more durable items remained in place. A huge plaster cast of the site was taken — it required 6 tons of plaster of Paris — and the archaeologists set to work to recover the artifacts. Whoever had been commemorated by the grave, he was clearly of the greatest

Far left:

Carefully reconstructed, the great iron helmet decorated with gilt is a powerful and dramatic monument to the Dark Age warrior who once wore it. Although scholars continue to speculate, his identity remains a mystery, and it is by no means certain that his body itself was interred at Sutton Hoo.

Below:

In Britain, all treasures found in the ground must be judged by an inquest to decide whether they are 'treasure trove', legally ownerless and therefore the property of the Crown, from which the finder is entitled to a percentage of the value. In August 1939, this inquest was convened to examine one of the most dramatic finds in British history, the Saxon ship-burial at Sutton Hoo, Suffolk.

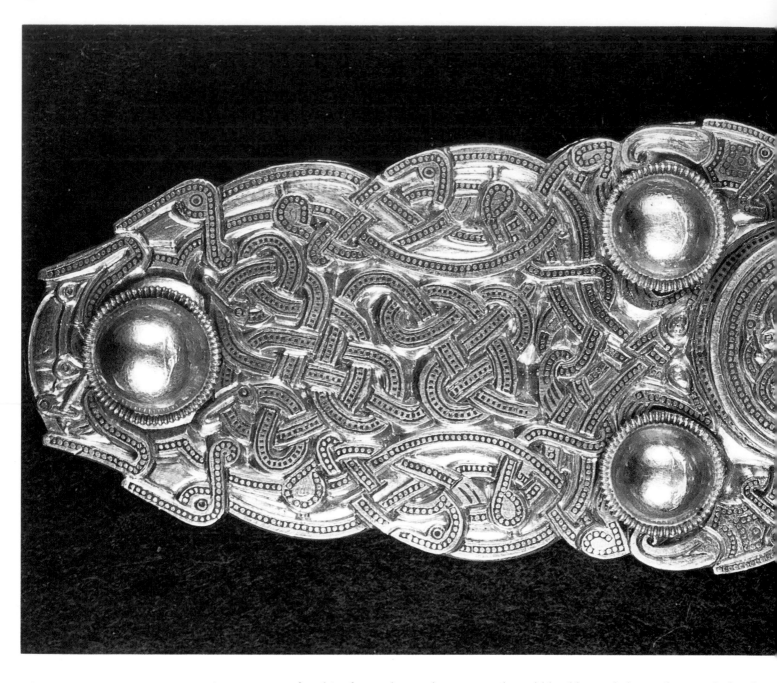

Above:

The great gold buckle from the Sutton Hoo burial. Solid gold, it weighs over 14 oz and is just over 5 inches long. It is decorated with a pattern of intertwined snakes, typical of the robust, chunky artistic style of the period.

importance, for his funeral goods were extraordinarily rich. There were great silver plates, buckled by the weight of the soil over the centuries but otherwise in excellent condition, iron goods and weapons, the silver tips and bases of great ceremonial drinking horns, and the remains of the man's personal costume. There were corroded iron fragments from a war helmet, later reconstructed. It was a fearsome piece, with hanging cheek guards and a face mask that covered the whole head, decorated with beautiful gilt dragon motifs. There was the central boss of a huge shield, similarly decorated, and the remains of a sword and scabbard. Most impressive, however, were

the gold buckles and clasps, decorated after the artistic fashion of the time with robust, swirling patterns, set with garnets and picked out with colored glass. There were the fittings of a magnificent purse, still containing over 30 gold coins and small ingots.

Experts have used these to date the burial at about AD 625. In addition to these most obvious treasures, there was a no less impressive iron standard, and a stone scepter, decorated with carved faces and mounted with an iron ring bearing the device of a stag in bronze, further proof of the importance and rank of the man buried there.

Later investigations

Curiously enough, however, despite this panoply, no trace of a body was found. It was suggested that the tomb might have been purely commemorative, the last tribute paid to a leader who died in the many battles of the time and whose body was never recovered. The outbreak of World War II prevented further examination. The treasures were removed, the hollow became overgrown with bracken, and the site was given to the army, who used the mounds as a tank obstacle course! Years later, however, the Sutton Hoo site was reopened, found to have survived even these trials with few after effects, and investigated again, using more sophisticated scientific techniques. Sufficient traces were found in the sandy, acid soil to suggest that a body might have been present after all, and that the skeleton had rotted away. The identity of the occupant still remains the subject of some conjecture. He was clearly a man of importance, possibly even Raedwald, a king of East Anglia.

One thing is certain, however. The Sutton Hoo site is the most complete example of a ship burial likely to be found, better even than the famous Scandinavian Viking examples at Gokstad and Oseberg, which, dramatic though they were, had been plundered in ages past.

Above:
The shoulder clasp from the cape of a king of long ago, part of the panoply buried with him when he was laid to rest in a wooden longship at Sutton Hoo in about AD 625. Most of the personal ornaments were of gold set with garnets and colored glass.

Albion's treasures

The British Isles are littered with the physical evidence of a past that stretches back beyond recorded history. Standing stones, stone circles, stone avenues, grassed-over burial mounds, and ancient hill forts are scattered over the countryside and, since the gradual spread of learning awakened an interest in antiquities, all have evoked wonder and conjecture. The world-famous circles of standing stones at Stonehenge and Avebury led to a fascination with that mysterious fraternity, the Druids of pre-Roman times. In the 18th and 19th centuries it was fashionable to attribute almost all prehistoric sites to the influence of the Druids. Although this view is no longer held, the Druids are a dark and intriguing presence at the beginning of British history. Before the birth of serious archaeology, when the distinction between fact and legend was less clear, more than one enthusiast was prompted to search for treasures of the past that are now thought to be no more than wishful thinking.

Digging for myths

In 1776, for example, the Duke of Northumberland attempted an excavation of Silbury Hill in Wiltshire, at 130 ft high one of the largest and most mysterious man-made hills in Europe. The Duke imported skilled tin miners from Cornwall, who dug an 8-ft square shaft from the top of the hill right down to the original ground level below. What he hoped to find was a life-size statue of one King Zel, on his horse, crafted in solid gold. Since King Zel seems to have been entirely mythical, it is not surprising that he found nothing — nor, indeed, did a rather more learned excavation in the 1960s. The purpose of Silbury remains outside the understanding of modern man.

Another character from Britain's legendary past who continues to attract attention is King Arthur. Numerous castles, hills, dark crags, and lakes carry legends associating them with the golden age of Arthur and his Round Table, but in this case there does seem to be a slender historical justification. Arthur was not the medieval paragon of legend, but a warlord in the Dark Ages following the collapse of the Roman presence in Britain. His Camelot was not a stone palace of glittering towers, but in all probability a hilltop refuge of palisades and trenches. Cadbury Castle in Somerset is currently held to be the most likely contender.

Boudica, the Iron Lady

One famous story which might just bear archaeological fruit one day concerns the famous British warrior queen, Boudica, who, as Boadicea, has been romanticized in folklore as a formidable lady riding a chariot with scythes on the wheels. In fact, Boudica was the wife of a chieftain of the Iceni tribe, who lived in East Anglia in Roman times. The chieftain, Prasutagus, seems to have lived in uneasy alliance with the Romans, but when he died in about AD 60 he made the mistake of naming the Romans his joint heirs with his wife, Boudica, and his two daughters. No doubt he hoped by this to keep on good terms with the Romans, but in fact it had the opposite effect, for the Romans took it as a cue to rampage through Iceni lands. Dreadful insults were heaped upon the royal family, and Boudica,

strong lady that she was, led a revolt. Several tribes erupted with pent-up fury against the many injustices inflicted on them by the Romans. A large Roman town had been built to house colonizing veterans at Colchester, and Boudica's host swept down on it, overwhelming the defenders and destroying all with fire and sword. A Roman legion was caught on the march and annihilated. Mad with bloodlust, the rebel host marched on London. The bulk of the Roman army was away in Wales, mopping up the last Celtic resistance there, and the city lay undefended. Roman accounts speak of thousands of civilians being put to gory deaths by the vengeful Iceni. Indeed, archaeological investigations have uncovered a pile of severed heads from the strata relating to this period.

But a reckoning was inevitable — the absent Roman legions marched back from Wales and Boudica set out to meet them. A great final battle was fought in which the Iceni, although they had the advantage of numbers, were outfought by Rome's tough professionals and mercilessly slaughtered. The Romans put down the revolt with ruthless brutality, and Boudica herself became ill and died. She is thought to have taken poison. According to one Roman account, 'the Britons mourned her deeply, and gave her a rich burial.' Her grave has never been found, and even the site of the great battle remains a matter for dispute. It seems highly likely that the Romans would have tried everything, especially torture, to find the location of Boudica's grave and despoil it. Perhaps, just perhaps, it escaped them. Its discovery would certainly cause an archaeological sensation, and it is difficult not to speculate on the nature of such a 'rich burial'. It would presumably include the great gold torque she is said to have worn around her neck, silver coins minted by the Iceni (some of which have been recovered from other caches dating from the rebellion), and also, very likely, the choicest of the loot her followers took from the great Roman towns they sacked and ravaged.

Treasures of the Maya

Right:
Catherwood and Stephens were
interested in the lost cities of the
Maya, and Edward Thompson
relished the gold artifacts he
dredged up from the well at
Chichén Itzá. But today it is
engraved stone inscriptions,
such as this stele, which attract
treasure hunters.

Far right:
A remarkable and rare Mayan
tomb beneath the Temple of
Inscriptions, Palenque. Mayan
script is still largely undeciphered,
but recent discoveries suggest that
high-ranking Maya may have
been buried with valuable grave
goods. Golden artifacts of Aztec
design from the north as well as
indigenous Mayan work were
recently found at one site.

Of the pre-Columbian peoples of America, perhaps the Maya remain the most mysterious. From AD 400 to 1000, their civilization flourished in the Yucatán peninsula, across the countries of modern Mexico, Belize, Guatemala, Honduras, and El Salvador. It produced spectacular cities which still bear testimony to a remarkable religious, artistic, and scientific life, and yet, by the time the Spanish conquistadores arrived in 1517, Mayan society had undergone such changes that it appeared to be in an advanced state of decay. Repeated military expeditions, and the introduction of European diseases to which the Maya had no natural resistance, completed the process. Thousands of Maya died and their culture collapsed. For centuries, their magnificent temples were overrun by the encroaching jungle. Occasionally a passing European adventurer would seek them out, marvel at their decaying splendor, and then move on. For the most part they were largely forgotten — until, that is, they were uncovered by the pioneering work of John Lloyd Stephens and Frederick Catherwood in the mid-19th century.

First sites discovered

Stephens was an American lawyer and diplomat who had travelled widely in Asia and the Middle East, and had developed a passion for ruins. Catherwood was a self-effacing English artist, whose sketches of Jerusalem attracted Stephens while he was on a visit to London. The two decided to team up to investigate tales of lost cities in the Central American jungles.

Their expeditions were brief — from 1839 to 1841 — but their adventures were varied, and the impact of their discoveries was enormous. At a time when travelling was difficult and the political situation volatile, to say the least, Stephens and Catherwood rediscovered three of the most breathtaking of the Mayan sites: Cópan, in Honduras, and Palenque and Chichén Itzá in Mexico. Catherwood made remarkably accurate drawings of Mayan buildings, idols, and inscriptions, and their publication was greeted with rapturous enthusiasm. His sketches of

great pyramids, overgrown with tangled bush and lianas, complex temples with trees growing from detritus on their wide flights of stone steps, and statues smothered in rapacious greenery, were largely responsible for the aura of romance which continues to surround the 'lost cities of the Maya'.

Proofs of human sacrifice

One man who was certainly inspired by them, a generation later, was a New Englander, Edward Thompson, who first sought out the ruins to further his theory that the Maya might be the origin of the legend of Atlantis. He soon dropped that idea, but was intrigued instead by rumors that the Mayan and Toltec inhabitants of Chichén Itzá made sacrifices, of both people and valuables, to a rain god, Yum Chac. This god inhabited a ceremonial well, or *cenote*, connected by a well-worn path to the central temple complex. The *cenote* itself was roughly oval, formed naturally by collapsing limestone strata, and was some 180 ft across. The rocky sides fell 80 ft to the green, unappetizing surface of the water below.

The depth of the water was anybody's guess, but Thompson resolved to find out, and to test the veracity of the legend by seeking any offerings which might remain at the bottom. He obtained an antiquated mechanical scoop and in 1904, with the aid of some local workers, began to dredge. At first it seemed he was doomed to be disappointed. Scoop after scoop revealed nothing but foul-smelling sludge, rotting vegetation and the remains of the odd animal that had fallen in and drowned. And then, as he was on the verge of giving up, Thompson scooped out a ball of copal resin, a substance known to have been used by the Maya in their religious ceremonies. More copal emerged, then a spear-throwing stick, and finally, to Thompson's delight, some human remains, indicating that the legend of human sacrifice was true. Thompson also dredged up gold — small bells, with their clappers removed to 'kill' them before sacrifice, and jewelry, a golden tiara. When the scoop could retrieve no more. Thompson descended in a deepsea diving suit and searched the floor of the well himself. By the time he had finished, a friend estimated that his finds were worth several hundreds of thousands of dollars at bullion rates alone. Thompson smuggled his treasure back to the Peabody Museum at

Harvard which had sponsored him, an unwise move which outraged the Mexican authorities and led to the closure of the site. After years of legal wrangling, some of the treasure was returned to Mexico, where the authorities themselves made two efforts — in 1961/1962 and 1967 — to explore the *cenote*, raising a further 2,600 items. And the Maya continue to intrigue. As recently as 1985, an American team working in Belize discovered a Mayan tomb dating from the time just before the Spanish Conquest. Not only did it contain gold items of apparently Aztec origin; it was of such splendor that it obliged scholars to reassess what they knew of relationships between the Central American peoples and of the influence of the Maya in their period of decline.

The mystery of the Temple

An astonishingly convoluted story of fabulous buried treasure from ancient times comes out of a little church at Rennes-le-Château in the south of France. The village lies some 30 miles south of Carcassonne and in earlier days was called Aereda. The Visigoths, who once ruled southern France and part of Spain, made a last stand there in AD 501 before being routed by the Franks. The village was then abandoned and became a ruin. When it was rebuilt much later it was renamed Rennes-le-Château.

In the 1800s, a shepherd wandering near the village stumbled across the entrance to a cave in the hillside. He was chasing a straying lamb into the cave and all at once found himself surrounded by dozens of skeletons and chests crammed with gold coins. The shepherd was understandably terrified, but not too scared to fill his pockets with all the coins he could carry before he made his way home. Rather unwisely, he could not resist telling people in the village how he had come by his serendipitous wealth, but refused to reveal the location of the cave. The villagers ridiculed such a patent fiction and had him executed for theft.

Nothing more was heard of the treasure for some years. Then, in 1885, a new parish priest arrived in the village. His name was Bérenger Saunière. He soon became a very close friend of a neighbor's teenage daughter, Marie Denarnaud, and from that time she became his inseparable companion, helping him to run the church and the parish.

Priceless parchments

In 1891, Bérenger put some restoration work in hand on the altar and the roof of the church, with the aid of a grant. Babon, the stonemason working on the job, found that one of the altar pillars was hollow, and inside it were hidden some wooden, wax-sealed rolls. When Bérenger opened one of these he found in it a parchment written in Latin and French.

Bérenger spent some time studying all the parchments. When the mayor turned up demanding to know what the parchments were all about, Bérenger, realizing that the man would not be able to understand them, showed them to him, explaining that they were useless documents concerning the Revolution. Suddenly, Bérenger put a stop to all restoration work. He left some of the parchments in Paris with experts on ancient manuscripts. From the ones he kept to himself he gleaned enough to send him hastily to the Louvre, where he bought a copy of a painting by Nicolas Poussin called 'Shepherds in Arcadia'. When he got back to his village, he was convinced that a

Right:
The little village of Rennes-le-Château, in southern France, was the scene of bitter fighting in centuries past. Today its fame rests largely on the astonishing wealth suddenly and secretly acquired by its originally unassuming parish priest around the turn of the century. Nobody has for certain solved the mystery of this ecclesiastical windfall, but rumor has it that the cleric stumbled on some of the treasure taken from Jerusalem by the Knights Templar.

treasure lay beneath the church. He told Marie about it, and together they tried to find it.

The instructions in the parchments were anything but straightforward. There were measurements in fathoms, leading from the altar, and references to a particular grave in the churchyard. Bérenger and Marie eventually managed to decipher the peculiar inscriptions on the gravestone and, in conjunction with further instructions, began to dig. They seem to have calculated correctly because they soon found the lost treasure vault.

Bérenger prospers

Suddenly, from being virtually a pauper, Bérenger seemed to have untold wealth at his fingertips. The church restoration was resumed on a far grander scale, with the priest paying

Right:
A shaft of sunlight illumines the inside of the dome of the Church of the Holy Sepulchre in Jerusalem. This was one of the holy places in Palestine that the Crusaders, together with 20,000 fighting Knights Templar, liberated and restored to Christianity. The Knights Templar were the richest and most powerful of all the medieval warrior orders, and at one time owned more than 8,000 castles. Many of these were spread throughout France and it is rumored that vast fortunes still lie hidden in some of them.

for it all out of his own pocket. All kinds of welcome and expensive amenities were added to the village, and Marie lived in high style, entertaining the cream of local society. It is thought that Bérenger shrewdly disposed of quantities of the treasure in various parts of Europe. But he was also careful to keep the location secret by assiduously defacing the clues on the gravestone.

As Bérenger continued to buy property and land, he put it all in Marie's name. Both the mayor and the bishop of Carcassonne called on Bérenger to demand an explanation for this sudden wealth. The priest wined and dined them extravagantly, explaining that he had inherited his riches from a recently deceased relative. When he reinforced this story with a persuasive parting bribe, both worthy gentlemen seemed to be satisfied.

In 1897, Bérenger built himself an enormous villa, in which he installed himself in great luxury at a reputed cost of 1 million francs. But by now a new bishop had taken over. He was made of sterner stuff and, disbelieving the old priest's tale, eventually had him suspended from office. When a new parish priest arrived in the village, Bérenger simply ignored him and the bishop, and carried on as usual, supported by his ecstatic villagers.

In January 1917, he paid out 8 million francs for a water supply to be laid on for Rennes-le-Château. It was his last act of beneficence because a few days later he died, of cirrhosis of the liver. Marie became the sole beneficiary of the mysterious treasure.

Marie probably never revisited the hidden vault; she had more than enough money to last for the rest of her life. For about a quarter of a century thereafter, she shut herself away. But in 1946 she confided the whole story to a Monsieur Corbu and his wife, who came to live with her. She eventually bequeathed her house to them and said she would tell them where the treasure lay just before she died. Regrettably, on 18th January 1953, Marie, by that time in her eighties, fell into a coma and died without recovering consciousness.

Clues point to Poussin's painting
There is no shortage of clues as to the location of the vault. Among the deciphered parchments one reads: 'This treasure belongs to Dagobert II, King, and to Sion, and he is here dead.' The code in the second parchment proved to be

Above:
*'Shepherds in Arcadia', painted
by the French artist Nicolas
Poussin, may contain a vital clue
to a vast treasure hoard hidden
at Rennes-le-Château. Poussin
depicts shepherds kneeling
at a tomb.*

astonishingly complex, but the message eventually read: 'Shepherdess no temptation to which Poussin Teniers hold the key peace 681 by the cross of this horse of God I complete this daemon guardian at midday blues apples.' It is a perfect anagram of the inscription on the headstone which Bérenger had been at such pains to scrub out. Unknown to him, the text had previously been copied and published before he began to cover his trail.

Poussin's painting corresponds almost exactly with the view from Rennes-le-Château. And there were other clues which indicated that Poussin was linked in some way with the secret. An American author, Henry Lincoln, who has made this mystery a life study, has unearthed much more significant material. He discovered, for example, that King Dagobert II was one of the last monarchs of the Merovingian dynasty. He was able to trace a direct link from the Franks (over whom

VOUS TOUS QUI SOUFFREZ QUI ETES ACCABLES ET JE VOUS S

Dagobert reigned) back to the Roman destruction of Jerusalem in AD 70. The Romans carried off the fabulous treasure of King Solomon's Temple. Could the hoard discovered by the unfortunate shepherd and later by Bérenger and Marie be the whole or part of the Jerusalem treasure? In spite of tempting clues pointing strongly in that direction, Lincoln thinks not. He believes there is much stronger evidence linking the treasure with the mystical Order of Rosicrucians and the secrets of alchemy. He is convinced that Bérenger

underwent a dramatic change of belief, secretly abandoning his faith for something akin to devil worship. Lincoln suggests that Bérenger's riches did not come from buried treasure but from resources supplied to him by the Priory of Sion, in other words by the Rosicrucians.

Opposing this theory is the testimony of Marie, who steadfastly averred that the vault existed and was still well supplied with treasure. Meanwhile, others speculate that Bérenger's wealth came from a more banal source — illegal sales of masses for the dead.

Above:

This painting faces the altar in the church at Rennes-le-Château. The church and churchyard abound with clues to the site of a massive treasure hoard: possibly one is contained in this painting, but the mystery has not been solved.

The legacy of the Jesuits

Treasure scented with a whiff of ecclesiasticism has been most prominently linked with that militant religious order, the Society of Jesus, popularly known as the Jesuits. The order was founded in 1534 by St Ignatius Loyola, and approved six years later by Pope Paul III. Pledged to a life of poverty, chastity, and obedience, the Jesuits rapidly grew in power and prestige both politically and economically.

King Philip II of Spain, uneasy at what he saw as a threat, curbed their control of wealth in Spain by means of a law passed in 1592. But Jesuit missionaries merely fanned out farther afield, concentrating particularly on the New World. This meant a vast region of Spanish colonies stretching from Colorado in the north to Bolivia in the south. In many of these areas mineral wealth was abundant. The Jesuits established missions and mines in all these places, seeking to save the souls of the uncivilized Indians who lived there and recruiting a convenient labor force to extract gold and silver from under the ground.

When the Spanish Crown got to hear of this bonanza, it not unnaturally wanted its cut, and promptly slapped a 20 percent tax (known as the Royal Fifth) on all New World takings. The reaction of the missionaries was predictably less than half-hearted and soon they were operating many ingenious fiddles to outwit the treasury. Things got so bad that a break was inevitable. Many prudent Jesuits began to hoard piles of silver and gold instead of sending it back to Europe, and were content to await the outcome. Finally, the Spanish Crown lost all patience and in 1767 expelled the order from Latin America. Before the missionaries left the New World (hoping doubtless to return before long) they carefully camouflaged the various caves, vaults, and other hiding places that concealed their

continuously amassed treasure. The expulsion order of 1767 also applied in Spain, Portugal, and France, and six years later the Society of Jesus was completely suppressed. It was not revived until 1814.

From that time onward, rumors and legends of huge hoards of Jesuit treasure lying in many parts of North and South America spread like prairie fires. Various expeditions have gone forth looking for this wealth, but so far as is known, not one of them has been rewarded with success.

Particularly persistent rumors have circulated about a magnificent silver mine discovered in 1736 and judged to be located somewhere in Arizona. The mine was called La Purísima Concepción and was said to lie slightly south of the Cerro Ruido Mountains. In 1750, the local Indians revolted, burned down the local mission, and threw out the Spanish authorities. But four years later,

it seems, the mine was reopened.

A rancher recently unearthed some ancient documents relating to the mine. They describe in detail the mine itself, but unfortunately hazy in precise instructions as to its whereabouts. Among other things they pinpoint La Purísima Concepción in relation to a Guadelupe mine, but there are many mines bearing that title all over the Southwest. The measurements, too, are unclear. But there are strong hints that the mine lies not far from the Tumacacori mission, a protected national monument on the east bank of the Rio Santa Cruz about 48 miles south of Tucson.

Indian legends tell of a rich mine somewhere in the 6,000-ft Cerro Ruido Peak. Not long after the end of World War I, two unnamed army veterans decided to do some prospecting there. They parted company for a few days while one man set off to explore Tucson and the other stayed on the mountain.

Above:

A spectacular storm over Tucson, Arizona, lights up the sky. Such storms not uncommonly cause flash floods in the hills and completely change the face of the landscape in a matter of hours. Treasure hunters, having pinpointed the location of a possible hoard in a derelict mine, have returned after a violent storm to find all their familiar landmarks completely obliterated.

Above:
These 17th-century church carvings were executed by unlettered Guaraní Indians in Paraguay, under the supervision of Jesuit instructors.

toiling for some hours on the debris below the ledge, he had finally uncovered the entrance to a cave carved out of the rock. The following day he entered the cave and found himself in a long, dark, dusty tunnel which he reckoned to extend to about 400 ft. By the light of his carbide lamp he could make out the outline of a heap of sacks against the wall. He opened one sack and found it held crude silver ore. At a rough estimate, he guessed there might be as much as 30 tons of the stuff lying there. He also noted that there were several smaller tunnels leading off the main one.

Deciding to leave things as they were until his friend returned, the man spent the next day exploring another canyon. There he suddenly came across a small opening covered with dried vegetation. Beyond it, in a clearing, stood the ruins of an ancient small church. It was crumbling and overgrown, but the man realized that it must be the remains of an old mission, probably linked to the mine he had stumbled on the previous day.

He photographed the scene, then made camp for the night. He was quite unable to get to sleep, however, because of some nameless dread that seemed to envelop him. This grew stronger by the minute until it reached the proportions of terror. Suddenly a ghastly scream echoed down the canyon. The man waited no longer. In sheer panic he leapt to his feet and raced back to his main campsite by the mine, crashing into boulders and tearing his clothes on thorns and bushes. Completely worn out, he collapsed under a tree and lay there until woken by his companion.

His friend dismissed the whole story as a nightmare, but the man insisted that he had not been dreaming and promised he could prove it when the film in his camera was developed. But the exciting silver mine obviously took priority. They removed a sample of the ore, and the nightmare man again elected to stay behind while his friend travelled once more into Tucson to have the sample assayed. He also took the camera with him to have the film developed.

As this man left the mountain, he became aware of a tremendous storm brewing up behind him. He turned and, using up the last remaining frame on the film roll, snapped a picture of the storm clouds over the Cerro Ruido. The assay was completed. Deeply disturbed by reports of floods and other storm

When they next met, the man who had stayed behind told his friend that he had found what appeared to be man-made excavations of some kind. The two of them examined the piles of rocks and dirt at the bottom of a ledge but, because they were running short of supplies, one of them volunteered to go into Nogales to restock. When he got back he found his friend asleep under a tree, his body scratched and his clothing torn.

His friend told him a fantastic story. After

havoc in the mountains, the man rushed back to look for his friend. On the way he collected the prints from the camera but didn't bother to look at them. He found the landscape quite drastically changed, with landslides, rock falls, and obliterated trails all adding to the confusion. He searched in vain for his companion. In spite of weeks of effort, with the help of teams from Nogales, no trace of him was ever found.

When eventually the survivor came to examine the photographs, he found pictures of the ruins of the old mission, just as his companion had described, and another of the cave entrance to the lost mine. There was also his own picture of the storm clouds over the Cerro Ruido. Years later, in 1958, he appeared on television to confirm the story, but still insisted on remaining anonymous. The lost mine and the mission are still there, presumably, for the finding.

Above:
Part of the restored altar in an 18th-century church at Concepción, Bolivia. The church was founded by the Jesuits during their missionary drive in the New World.

5

The Spoils of War

For the past 3,000 years or so, the taking of spoils in the form of precious objects has been the privilege of conquerors, both to aggrandize themselves and to reward their followers. By the same token, the conquered have tried to conceal their valuables as insurance against uncertain days ahead. This millennia-old game of hide-and-seek provides us with some of the most fascinating lost treasures of the world, and also some of the most spectacular treasures to have been found. The hunt takes us from the warrior-horsemen of ancient Thrace, on the shores of the Black Sea, to the Germany of Adolf Hitler.

The Thracian civilization was established in and around present-day Bulgaria by about 3500 BC, and there is evidence that it was working locally mined gold at that time — after Egypt, perhaps the oldest known culture to do so. Certainly, by about 500 BC, the Thracians were producing magnificent gold and silver artifacts that had no contemporary equivalent anywhere. Most of those so far found come from tombs and graveyards, but in 1985/1986, a new hoard came to light in the village of Rogozen, in northwest Bulgaria, in unusual circumstances. For the 165 silver gilt items found were not associated with a grave. Initial investigation suggested that they had been buried sometime after the middle of the 4th century BC, at the time when Philip II of Macedon (father of the famous Alexander) was conquering Thrace. The inference is that they were hidden from the invaders by a chieftain later killed or captured in battle with the Greeks — one of the earliest known concealments of riches for such reasons.

Golden ark

Another may have taken place more than 150 years previously, in what is now Israel and Jordan, and if that treasure were to be found it could be the most spectacular discovery of all time — worth a staggering $900 million or more, according to some experts. In 586 BC, King Nebuchadnezzar of Babylon stormed Jerusalem, sacking the city and its Temple of Solomon and carrying the Jews off into captivity. But there is evidence that before the Babylonians arrived the Jews managed to conceal or spirit away a great deal of their secular and religious wealth, perhaps even including the long-sought golden Ark of the Covenant, in which the most sacred Jewish writings were kept.

Evidence to this effect is adduced by authors such as René Noorbergen from

Left:
A mounted warrior depicted on part of a silver-gilt helmet dating from the 4th century BC found in Romania. A number of treasure hoards, possibly the pillage of conquerors, have been found in the Balkans, an area many times overrun by invading armies.

Below:
The Corbridge Lion, a 2nd-century AD stone fountain head carved in the shape of a lion attacking a deer. It was unearthed at the Roman fort of Corstopitum, near Corbridge, Northumberland, England, where many Romano-British artfacts have been found.

materials recovered from Qumran, where the religious writings known as the Dead Sea Scrolls were accidentally discovered in 1947. The materials on which Noorbergen draws are not part of the scrolls, but were found some five years later, and are engraved on thin copper sheets rather than parchment. Translated, they list, according to Noorbergen and his fellow writer John Marc Allegro, 61 sites in the Holy Land where treasure is buried, including a total of nearly 97,000 lb of gold and 338,000 lb of silver (the full list is in Noorbergen's *Treasures of the Lost Races*). There is nothing to connect this list with Nebuchadnezzar's invasion other than surmise, but the case for doing so appears plausible. Unfortunately, the descriptions of the sites are very vague. One account reads: 'There is a money chest in the fortress in the Vale of Anchor containing 17 talents [a talent is about 75 lb, hidden 40 cubits under the steps of the eastern entrance'. As yet, nobody has succeeded in relating the descriptions

Right:
Six Celtic torques, or neck rings,
found at Ipswich, Suffolk, in
eastern England. Although the
designs are all broadly similar,
each example is slightly different,
perhaps reflecting the individual
preferences of the original owners,
members of the warrior class.

Below:
This beautiful 16th-century
miniature — a treasure in its own
right — shows the Mongol hordes
of Genghis Khan besieging an
unnamed Chinese town during
Genghis' all-conquering career.
The miniature comes from a
history compiled in Persia and
completed in 1596.

sufficiently closely to the modern landscape to find any of the caches.

Luck, sometimes assisted by intelligent guesswork, has played a large part in the discovery, for example in Britain, France, and elsewhere, of hoards buried by wealthy Romans as their western empire crumbled under the barbarian onslaughts between about AD 161 and AD 476. There were no written records to lead investigators to caches such as England's Mildenhall Treasure or the many Roman items of the 4th century found piecemeal since 1731 at Corbridge on the River Tyne. Plenty more hoards of this period must exist in Europe, although there are few clues to where precisely they are.

According to various legends, the barbarian hordes that raided or conquered Roman centers of civilization left behind lots of treasure. Alaric, leader of the Visigoths who sacked Rome in 410, is said to have pillaged virtually all of the city's treasure. Attila the Hun, who died in 453 and was another scourge of the collapsing western empire, is supposed to have acquired great wealth during his campaign in the Balkans. The 12th-century epic poem *Nibelunglied*, in which Attila appears as Etzel, speaks both of the treasures he owned and of his insatiable greed for more. No one knows what these treasures may have been, nor where they are now. Similar tales attached themselves to Genghis Khan and his grandson

Left:
*This magnificent example of an
Iron Age torque adorned a Celtic
warrior in Britain during the 1st
century BC. It is made from
electrum, an alloy of gold and
silver, and was found at Ken Hill,
near Snettisham in Norfolk,
England. The torque is now on
display at the British Museum
in London.*

Kublai Khan, whose Mongol followers overran much of Central Asia and threatened the portals of Eastern Europe in the 13th century, and to Tamerlane, who emulated their feats in Southern Asia from 1369. However, here we are on somewhat surer ground. The Venetian traveller Marco Polo described at first hand the wonders of Kublai Khan's summer capital of Shang-tu (the Xanadu of poetry and myth), including an entire hillside decorated with semi-precious lapis lazuli to delight the Khan's eye. Since the mid-19th century, explorers and archaeologists have been investigating the Mongol territories, making some spectacular finds. But they have not yet traced the treasure hoard of Genghis Khan, said to lie somewhere in the arid steppes of Central Asia, nor the gold and other valuables of Tamerlane, hidden outside his capital city of Samarkand.

The records of the monks

The spread of Christianity throughout Western Europe contributed, as a by-product, to our knowledge of the treasures pillaged by marauders in the first millennium AD, for two reasons. The monasteries of the Dark and Middle Ages were the repositories of learning, the only places where written records of everyday events were kept, and many of those records have survived. And, as the monasteries and their associated churches grew richer, they became a natural focus for armies or

bands of raiders in search of booty.

Ecclesiastical accounts, for example, tell us a great deal about the depredations of the Vikings, whose longships terrorized the coasts of Britain, Ireland, and France from the 8th century onward, and eventually carried them into the Mediterranean and eastward to Constantinople. At Lindisfarne, off England's northeast coast, a surprise raid in AD 793 left the church 'despoiled of all its ornaments' — jeweled caskets, valuable statuary, rich vestments, and much more — according to

Above:
*The majestic ruins of Corfe Castle
dominate the countryside near
Wareham, Dorset, in southern
England. During the Civil War,
the owner, Lady Mary Bankes, is
said to have concealed the family
fortune in a well, which she then
blew up to prevent Cromwell's
troops from finding it.*

a very detailed contemporary report.

At Rouen in France in 841, the Vikings plundered the monasteries, slew the monks, and extorted gold and silver from the ordinary inhabitants as the price for their departure.

From the middle of the 9th century the Vikings raided Spain, Portugal, southern France, Italy, and the Arab lands of North Africa, looting and exacting tribute. Their first attacks came as a complete surprise, giving the victims little time to hide their most precious objects. Later, however, it seems some valuables were concealed, among them perhaps a gold-and-silver 8th-century chalice found at Ardagh in Ireland in 1868.

Legends of treasure hidden from the Vikings abound in Western Europe, but a bigger mystery surrounds the spoils they took, which must have amounted to a massive fortune over the years. The Frankish kings are recorded to have paid over 685 lb of gold and

43,000 lb of silver in tribute alone. The English contributed tens of millions of predominantly silver coins in Danegelt (a form of tax, levied as 'protection' against Viking raids), and lesser quantities of silver came from North Africa and from Germany. Little of this has been found.

A thousand or so relatively small hoards have been traced in Scandinavia, including some 60,000 coins of Arab silver and others of Frankish and English origin. The biggest Viking silver cache of all — weighing 88 lb and four times larger than any other — was unearthed at Cuerdale in northwest England in 1840, and was seemingly the war chest of a 10th-century leader. The largest gold cache of Viking origin, weighing just 10 lb, was found on an island in the River Shannon in Ireland in the 19th century. Some of the Vikings' booty must have been lost in shipwrecks such as the one off the Shetland Isles in 1151. Nevertheless, much still remains to be accounted for.

Right:

Robert the Bruce, King of Scotland and leader of the Scottish army that vanquished the English at Bannockburn in 1314, shortly afterward attended the consecration of the cathedral at St Andrews, where he gave thanks for his victory. According to legend, Robert left more tangible tokens of appreciation, too — a hoard of valuables taken from the defeated enemy. These are said to lie in a vault under the ruins.

Left:
US Private Ernest Garrison guards part of the looted art collection amassed by Hermann Goering, who acquired vast numbers of priceless paintings from all over Europe and displayed some of them at his home, Karinhall, in Berlin. Just before Germany's final defeat, the treasures were rushed by train to a secret cave near Königsee in the Bavarian Alps for safe keeping. But shortly afterward Goering revealed their hiding place to the US military.

Conquests and discoveries

Between 1095, when Pope Urban II preached the First Crusade to free Jerusalem from the Turks, and 1580, when Francis Drake completed his voyage around the world, the previously inward-looking Western Europeans spread their developing techniques of warfare across the globe, although this expansion did not prevent them from doing battle with each other at home. At the same time, as we have seen, stirrings in Asia threw up a succession of Mongol rulers whose names became synonymous with pillage.

The early part of this period saw the flowering of the feudal system, with powerful barons conducting their affairs from great castles and paying only nominal fealty to overlords and kings, while constantly vying with each other for riches and power. Their activities have given rise to many tales of hidden spoils. In Scotland, for example, hoards of valuable 14th-century coins hidden by warring leaders have come to light at Montrave and elsewhere, and another massive treasure is said to lie underground at Roslin Castle. The ruins of St Andrew's Cathedral reputedly guard an immense collection of booty captured from the defeated English at the Battle of Bannockburn in 1314.

But Europe's feudal struggles pale in comparison with the wholesale slaughter and pillaging that accompanied European colonization of the Americas, in particular by the Spaniards. Earlier chapters have recounted the history of the treasure fleets and the brutalities associated with the first searches for El Dorado. However, there are many who believe that the conquistadores succeeded in appropriating only a fraction of the gold and silver of the various civilizations they encountered, while much more was hidden.

For example, in 1971 investigators found a massive system of tunnels, more than 50 miles long, leading from Mount Huarascarán in the Peruvian Andes westward to the Pacific Coast. Tradition says the tunnels were used as an underground treasure store by the beleaguered Incas, though as yet no treasure has been discovered. One theory is that the tunnels originally continued beneath the ocean to the offshore island of Guanape, and that somewhere in this last stretch, now flooded, is a huge vault stacked with the Incas' wealth.

Another legend asserts that the Aztecs of Central America also tried to thwart the Spaniards by hiding their most prized possessions in remote jungle temples. Among them are, reputedly, 52 golden tablets comprising a history of Central America, somewhere in the region of Tenochtitlán.

Oliver Cromwell (1599-1658) and his Parliamentarian army survey the field of victory at Marston Moor during the English Civil War. The battle, in 1644, was the first defeat for Charles I's Royalist cavalry. England abounds in stories of treasures hidden during this troubled period of her history, when countless items of gold and silver were melted down to help finance the Royalist cause.

Civil wars and revolutions

The 17th and 18th centuries saw massive upheavals in the established order in Europe and some of its colonies, beginning with the Thirty Years' War of 1618-48 and the English Civil War of 1642-51, and culminating in the American and French revolutions of 1776 and 1789 respectively. During this epoch, however, attitudes towards pillage, in the west at least, began to change, though races regarded as 'inferior', such as those of South America and later Africa, remained fair game. So did vulnerable and valuable cargoes on the high seas. But Europe itself was not subject to depredations on the scale practiced by the likes of Alaric or the Vikings. Various factors contributed to this gradual evolution: the publication, by the Dutchman Hugo Grotius in 1625, of a treatise regarded as the foundation of the rules of war and of the settlement of international disputes; a more enlightened attitude, a product of the Age of Reason, toward the treasures of other nations; and the spreading use of paper money, whose value could be cancelled at the stroke of a pen.

None of this was immediately clear, of course, to those caught up in the English Civil War. The west of England and Wales, in particular, are reputed to house still unrecovered treasures hidden from the

Parliamentary forces of Oliver Cromwell. At Corfe Castle in Dorset a fortune is believed to lie at the bottom of a well, hurled there for safety by the owner, who then dynamited it over. On the Parliamentary side, John Barkstead, put in charge of the Tower of London by Oliver Cromwell, used the opportunity to extract all the valuables he could from the Royalist prisoners held there. Barkstead's spoils are thought to have been hidden in the Tower, but have not been found.

The two great revolutions in the last quarter of the 18th century began among what we would call today the middle classes, who were more concerned with political and civil rights than with the seizure of booty for its own sake. The American Revolution continued in that vein, and produced few tales of hidden treasures. The French Revolution and its immediate aftermath drew in the urban poor and at least some of the peasantry, but events such as the incursions into the palaces of Versailles and the Tuileries were marked more by wanton destruction and small-scale theft than by mass pillage. The same was eventually true of the Russian Revolution of 1917, although not of the civil war that followed.

Fleeing French aristocrats took what they could carry with them in the way of valuables — Marie-Antoinette, captured before she could

get out of France, had jewelry and a silver dinner service — and may have concealed more at home. Some French stately homes have unproven legends to that effect. But in general, relatively little disappeared without trace. This apparent restraint continued into the Napoleonic era. For still-missing treasures lost in war, we must look to our own century — in particular to the depredations of the Nazis — or outside Europe.

African hoard

The discovery of diamonds at Kimberley in the 1869 and gold on the Witwatersrand in 1886 brought prospectors, speculators, and adventurers flocking from all over the world to what is now South Africa, in search of their fortunes. Among them was the Englishman Cecil Rhodes. Rhodes' ambition was boundless, and in the mid-1880s his British South Africa Company succeeded in obtaining mining rights in Matabeleland (Ndebeland) from the local tribal chief, Lobengula.

Despite their agreement, relations between Rhodes and Lobengula soon grew sour, as it became clear that the Englishman intended to annex Matabeleland and its neighboring regions for the British crown. Before that, however, open warfare had broken out between the troops of Rhodes' company

and Lobengula's Matabele.

There is some evidence to show that the Matabele king had prepared for the conflict by instructing those of his subjects who flocked south for work in the mines to smuggle back what they could in the form of diamonds and gold. At any rate, Lobengula amassed a fortune — in bullion, coins, gold dust, diamonds, and ivory — valued at $14 million at the time. Inevitably the Matabele were defeated, but when Rhodes' troops entered the tribal capital of Bulawayo in 1893 there was no sign of Lobengula and only a small portion of the gold. Lobengula had apparently fled with the treasure up the valley of the Zambesi River, and simply disappeared, never to be seen again. Rumor said that he had hidden his wealth at the source of the Kori River, but an expedition in the 1920s failed to find the cache — perhaps because there are two waterways of the same name in the region and the wrong one was investigated. Some versions of the tale maintain that Lobengula, nearing death and deserted by all but a few loyal followers, chose to be walled up in a mountain cave with the treasure.

Above:
The Cuerdale hoard of Viking silver was found by 19th-century laborers shoring up the banks of the River Ribble in northwest England, and contained more than 7,000 coins, as well as fibulae (brooches), chains, and other items of jewelry.

An imperial fortune

Right:
The ill-starred Tsar Nicholas II (1868-1918) is said to have died at Ekaterinburg. However, the only item linked to him, and that tentatively, in the alleged mineshaft grave was a belt buckle. The absence of firm evidence of his death led to persistent speculation that he survived in anonymity, perhaps for years.

Right:
The last Tsarina of Russia, German-born Alexandra Feodorovna (1872-1918), contributed to the downfall of the Russian monarchy by the weight she attributed to the opinions of the peasant mystic Grigory Rasputin. Like the rest of the imperial family, Alexandra is said to have been murdered by the Bolsheviks in July 1918 at Ekaterinburg, and her remains cast into a mineshaft. Items belonging to her recovered from the mine included a cross of emeralds, diamonds, and pearls set in platinum.

The tangled events of the Russian Revolution of 1917 and the ensuing civil war between the Bolsheviks and their opponents, the White Army, have produced more tales of lost treasure than any other single chapter of 20th-century history. The thousands of aristocrats and prosperous merchants who fled abroad took what personal wealth they could carry with them, often claiming to have left fortunes in valuable items concealed at home against the possibility of returning later. In Russia, the armies of both sides as well as the fearsome bandit chiefs of Siberia, who owed allegiance to neither side, plundered deserted estates, banks, stores, and other buildings. In the case of the two armies, looted valuables were needed to sustain their war efforts; for the bandits, the motive was purely greed.

Many of these tales should be treated with extreme caution. Among the émigrés, pitchforked out of their previously comfortable existences, there were many who invented yarns of abandoned wealth, hoping to con the gullible and greedy into supporting them. However, there is considerable evidence to show that the most fabulous treasure of all did indeed exist, and that there is at least a reasonable possibility that a portion of it remains hidden somewhere.

The hoard is known by a variety of names — the Romanov gold, Kolchak's gold, the treasure of the White Army — and is commonly discussed as if it were one massive collection of platinum, gold, silver, jewels, and other items. In fact, it was three separate collections, and their fates, so far as is known, were completely different, although the second and third may to some extent have coalesced.

The fate of the Romanovs

The first represented the personal fortunes of the last Tsar, Nicholas II, and other members of the imperial Romanov family, together with jewelry belonging to the crown. The crown jewels were rapidly seized by the Bolsheviks; some were sold, and the rest are now on display in the Kremlin. The Romanovs' own fortune in Russia in 1917 amounted perhaps to $4 million. Some of it was used to pay the expenses of Nicholas, his wife, and children during their house arrest at Tobolsk and Ekaterinburg (now Sverdlovsk), and much of the rest was confiscated by the Bolsheviks. Items of the royal family's personal jewelry were found at Ekaterinburg after the Tsar and his immediate relatives were massacred there in 1918, according to the generally accepted version of events. Many people have challenged the account of the Ekaterinburg killings. Alternative versions spare the entire family, who then lived abroad incognito, or spare all save Nicholas himself, who may have been killed at Ekaterinburg or somewhere else, or allow Anastasia, the youngest crown princess, to escape. Claims in 1989/91 that all the bodies of all the family had been located were not authenticated.

That would seem to account for most of the Romanov effects in Russia itself. However, it is known that members of the family made deposits abroad in the years before World War I, and there are persistent reports of a fortune in gold lying in a bank somewhere outside Russia, awaiting a legitimate claimant. It was perhaps part of an attempt to obtain these deposits that led Anna Anderson, a German, and a number of other women to assert that they were the miraculously spared Anastasia, right up to the 1970s. Needless to say, all were regarded as impostors by surviving relatives of the Romanovs.

Some money does lie in a bank in East Berlin, but the collapse of the German mark between the wars made it virtually valueless. A more favored site for the gold is the Bank of England in London; however, bank officials have consistently denied that it is there. A possible explanation, for which there is historical evidence, is that deposits were made before 1914, but withdrawn in 1915.

The remains of the treasure

The second, and by far the larger, portion of the treasure consisted mainly of state funds, moved around by the White Army as it struggled against the Bolsheviks and supplemented by other valuables acquired in the towns where the army was temporarily stationed — among them Ekaterinburg, Perm, some 200 miles to the northwest, and Kazan, some 300 miles southwest of Perm. In the shifting tides of the Civil War, it is difficult if not impossible to keep close track of the treasure's movements.

However, there are reports of large quantities of gold and other valuables being captured by the Bolsheviks when they took Ekaterinburg, and then being transported by rail to Perm on 17th July 1918 — the day after the supposed massacre of the Romanovs and just before Ekaterinburg fell again to the Whites. This collection seems to have been a mixture of the Romanovs' personal wealth, state property, and appropriated gold. Part was found when the Whites recaptured Perm, but the rest disappeared, presumably moved by the Bolsheviks. At virtually the same time, Kazan capitulated to the Whites. Here too there was a vast treasure store, deposited before the Revolution to keep it from the invading Germans. The Bolsheviks had either not discovered it or been unable to move it. According to one account, it was worth more than $1 billion at contemporary values, and consisted of gold bullion, platinum, jewels, stocks, and bonds. This vast fortune, perhaps supplemented eventually by the prize from Perm, was moved eastward by rail, deep into the fastnesses of Siberia, where Admiral Alexander Kolchak, leader of the White Army and titular Supreme Ruler of All the Russias, had his headquarters.

Above:
The Grand Duchesses Olga and Tatiana, daughters of Nicholas and Alexandra, at work with other members of the imperial family in the grounds of the royal palace at Tsarskoe Selo, south of St Petersburg, in the first phase of their captivity. They dug up part of a lawn to make a vegetable garden. In August 1917, the royal prisoners were transferred to Tobolsk in Siberia, and in April 1918 they were moved again, to Ekaterinburg.

The Whites in retreat

Right:
Lake Baikal, in the heart of Siberia, lay on the White Army's line of retreat from Omsk. Its deep waters may conceal Tsarist bullion, although other accounts suggest the gold might have been hidden somewhere along its shores. Certainly, many fleeing Whites drowned in the lake.

Top far right:
Heavily armored trains called broneviki, *lumbering along the Trans-Siberian Railroad at 15 mph, played a major part in the Russian Civil War. This one, the* Orlik, *belonged to the Czech Legion, who allied themselves with the anti-Bolshevik White Army. The Czechs escorted Admiral Kolchak, and the Whites' treasure, on the retreat from Omsk toward Irkutsk.*

Far right:
Two members of the Czech Legion guard freight cars at Kurgan, west of Omsk on the Trans-Siberian Railroad. Some 50,000 Czechs were in Russian territory in 1918, fighting Austro-Hungary for the independence of their homeland. After World War I officially ended, the Czech Legion was virtually forced to join the Whites to try to obtain its passage home.

By November 1919, the Russian Civil War was two years old. The Red Army, welded by Leon Trotsky into a formidable fighting force, was advancing, while Admiral Kolchak's Whites, supported by the major Western powers, were in retreat eastwards along the Trans-Siberian Railroad from Omsk, their headquarters for the past year or so. With them, it is said, went a special train carrying the treasure, including a claimed 500 tons of gold (there must be considerable doubt whether that amount of bullion could even be moved by one train in those conditions).

Lost gold

Within a couple of months, Kolchak's reign was over. The Western allies had begun to court the Bolshevik government. Irkutsk, the central Siberian city earmarked as the Whites' next headquarters, had fallen to Bolshevik sympathizers. Kolchak had no choice but to surrender, yielding his mantle as 'supreme ruler' to General Denikin, who was still fighting the Reds in the south. Kolchak was tortured for several weeks, and finally shot, with many of his followers. Others managed to escape, but most froze to death trying to reach freedom. The gold, meanwhile, had disappeared somewhere in the 2,000 miles of Siberia between Omsk and Irkutsk.

Or so, at least, the story runs. As with the fate of the Tsar, there are many versions of what happened next. One is that the gold was not lost at all, but simply handed over to the Bolsheviks at Irkutsk by members of the Czech Legion that had associated itself with Kolchak, in return for their release. If that were the case, or if the Bolsheviks had found the gold in some hiding place, they were under no obligation to publicize the fact and may well have chosen not to do so.

On the other hand, rumor and tradition hold that the Bolsheviks did not obtain the treasure. Some argue that the remnants of the White Army kept it and tried to move it across the frozen waters of Lake Baikal, near Irkutsk, the deepest lake in the world; when the ice melted, the treasure plunged into the depths below. Others say it was hidden somewhere along the Trans-Siberian Railroad, in a disused mine or in the crypt of a ruined church, where it was stacked by soldiers who were subsequently shot to preserve the secret.

An alleged survivor of this incident, one Slava Bogdanov, reportedly returned to the site in 1959 with an American accomplice and removed ingots weighing 325 pounds. Bogdanov was killed by frontier guards trying to crash a roadblock, and his haul was seized, it is claimed, leaving the unknown American the sole person with knowledge of the cache. This part of the quest ends in a seemingly blank wall.

However, there remains the third portion of the treasure. While Kolchak was threatening the Bolsheviks from the east, Denikin was harassing them from the south. He too had need of a war chest, and may even at some stage have been given part of the imperial riches for that purpose. Certainly, he would have taken anything he could get from banks and abandoned private estates to pay his troops, buy provisions, transport, and weapons, and foment subversion.

A Black Sea cache

In 1973, in a book published in Paris, a Russian émigré, Nicholas Svidine, claiming to have served in Denikin's army, recounted events in southern Russia during the closing days of the Civil War in 1920 (that is when the Soviet Union says it finished; hostilities actually continued in Siberia for another two years). According to Svidine, Denikin realized defeat was imminent and therefore ordered treasure to be amassed to finance continuing guerilla resistance to be Bolsheviks or an eventual reinvasion of Russia. The booty was assembled and somehow transferred to Bulgaria, along the Black Sea coast, a destination for many fleeing Whites.

There it was temporarily concealed in a cellar before being divided into four caches and buried somewhere in wild woodland in the region of Bourgas, a major Black Sea port. So far as is known, it could still be hidden beneath the trees.

By all accounts, Denikin's treasure was not as impressive as that of Kolchak and was worth only about one-tenth as much — $100 million. Still, it represents a tidy fortune in thousands of gold roubles, foreign notes and coins, 450 pounds of platinum, baskets of cut and uncut gems, and stock certificates. In addition, there are said to be state documents revealing hitherto unknown facts about events during the Revolution and the Civil War; it is tempting to speculate that, if these papers really exist, they could contain clues to Kolchak's gold.

Svidine apparently made efforts to relocate and remove the treasure, but without success.

As a Soviet satellite after World War II, Bulgaria did not welcome treasure hunters. But the collapse of Communism in Eastern Europe may now allow Svidine's claims to be properly investigated.

King John's missing regalia

John, King of England from 1199 to 1216, is probably one of the most reviled monarchs in history, even though it was in his reign that the Magna Carta, a cornerstone of British freedom, was drawn up. His continuing power struggle with the barons, alleged responsibility for the murder of his nephew Arthur of Brittany, quarrels with the Pope, and unsuccessful military campaign in France all stain his rule. On top of that, he became the only English monarch to have lost the country's crown jewels in their entirety, setting off a treasure hunt that has gone on, without result, for more than 700 years.

The details of how the loss occurred are obscure, but the salient facts are known. In October 1216, John was once again in the middle of a dispute with his nobles, and a rebellion against his authority had broken out in the Midland counties. The King marched north from London to quell the uprising, accompanied by his loyal troops and a baggage train containing, among other things, his own royal regalia, and that of his grandmother, the Empress of Germany, and a sizeable fortune in gold and jewels. In the early part of the month the entourage halted at King's Lynn, an ancient port in what was then the richest area of England.

In those days, King's Lynn lay practically on the shores of the Wash, a broad, shallow North Sea inlet between Lincolnshire and Norfolk on the east coast. Its edges then were shifting, unpredictable banks of sand, liable to frequent flooding. On 12 October, the cumbersome baggage train set out across the sands, southwest to Wisbech for a rendezvous with John, who, it is thought, had gone there by a longer, but safer, route.

Swallowed by the sea

Somewhere on the sandbanks disaster struck. A fast-running tide engulfed men, horses, and the treasure. By some accounts, everything was lost; others say that many of the valuables were saved and hurriedly loaded onto rescue ships. Whatever the truth, none of the regalia, gold, or jewels was ever seen again. John himself died of a fever at Newark a few days later, practically penniless from the loss.

Since then, historians, archaeologists, and

Left:
This highly romanticized turn-of-the-century painting, now in the House of Commons in London, shows King John being presented with the Magna Carta by the English barons at Runnymede on the River Thames in 1215. Contrary to popular belief, John did not sign the document, but signaled his acceptance of its terms by affixing his seal. It brought him little respite, and by 1216 he was again at war with the barons in a campaign that cost him first his treasure and, shortly afterwards, his life.

Far left:
King John's Cup, displayed in King's Lynn, Norfolk, in eastern England, is often supposed to be part of the treasure the unfortunate monarch lost in the waters of the Wash. But expert examination has shown that it was made at least 70 years after his death.

treasure seekers have tried to work out the exact route the baggage train took on that fatal day, and therefore where the treasure itself may be. They have been hampered in their task because much of the southwest fringe of the Wash has been drained since the 13th century, including the possible paths the baggage train may have followed, and there is considerable disagreement over the likely site of the accident.

Seeking the lost trail

It seems reasonable to assume that the party headed first for one of the villages on the west bank of a tongue of dry land between the Great Ouse River and the Wellstream, a strip of water into which several rivers drain. That would have brought the baggage train to the villages of Cross Keys, Walpole or, the most southerly point, Walsoken. To reach the first two they would have had to cross the sandbanks at the mouth of the Great Ouse. If Walsoken was the immediate destination, they

could have crossed the Great Ouse estuary at a narrow point higher up, and made most of the journey on land.

Whichever staging post was chosen, the Wellstream had to be forded to arrive in Wisbech, and it too was flanked by shifting sandbanks. This seems the most likely place for the disaster, but treasure seekers still have to find the exact spot within an almost triangular area measuring some 10 miles from base to apex and some 5 miles across at the widest point. It has defeated them for seven centuries, and becomes harder as the land is developed and increasingly built up.

Legend says that one item of the treasure was salvaged, and it is on display in the Guildhall of the Holy Trinity in King's Lynn. The richly gilded, embossed, and enameled vessel is known as King John's Cup. In its own right, it is a priceless example of medieval craftsmanship, but the style and content of the enameled panels show that it was made between 70 and 150 years after John's death.

When the Romans withdrew

At the end of the 4th century AD, the western Roman Empire was beginning to crumble under the combined weight of barbarian onslaughts and internal dissension. Troops from far-flung outposts were recalled to help man frontiers nearer to Rome. In Britain, the imperial forces departed in AD 407, leaving the country vulnerable to Saxons from across the North Sea, who had been eyeing it greedily, and periodically raiding it, for several decades.

By about 600, the Saxons had conquered and settled much of present-day England and lowland Scotland, despite resistance by Romano-British leaders of whom the legendary Arthur was almost certainly one. But in the early days of the Saxon raids it was by no means apparent that Britain would be overrun. The Romano-British in the most vulnerable areas fled from their town houses, villas, and farms — some to the fastnesses of Wales and the West Country. Often, they concealed those treasures they could not carry with them, fully intending to reclaim them later when the Saxon threat had been dealt with.

A pattern of concealment

From sites in Britain and elsewhere in Europe, we know these caches followed a pattern. In general, they were made at some distance from the buildings where the valuables originated, presumably to make them harder for the invaders to find; burial in the ground seems to have been the preferred method of concealment. At two of the richest British villas dating from this period — Lullingstone in Kent and Chedworth in Gloucestershire — no gold or silver items have been found, although there are lavish mosaics and murals, and plenty of semi-precious and everyday objects. On the other hand, a hoard of 4th-century silverware discovered at Water Newton in East Anglia is not associated with any building of the period in the immediate vicinity. So unearthing Roman treasure hidden from the barbarians is largely a matter of luck. Certainly, luck played a large part in the discovery of the most important collection of Roman works of art yet found in Britain. It breaks our general rule, in that part of the site was no more than 30 yards from a 4th-century building.

A plowman's fortune

In 1942, a plowman working in the fields near Mildenhall in Suffolk decided, for reasons unclear to us, to set his plowshare deeper than usual. As the plow broke soil that had probably been untouched for centuries, it turned up an assortment of encrusted objects that appeared, when some of the earth was knocked away, to be made of lead or pewter, and therefore of little intrinsic value. The plowman handed these objects over to his employer, who took them home and, with a remarkable lack of curiosity, thought little more about the matter.

But in 1946, the discovery was officially reported and the objects were properly cleaned. The Mildenhall Treasure was revealed in all its magnificence — 34 pieces of priceless decorated silverware, of fine quality and almost perfectly preserved. Most date from the 4th century, but some are almost 200 years older, perhaps family heirlooms handed down through the generations. The majority came from Rome or Gaul, with a few that may have been of local British manufacture.

There are goblets, dishes, and spoons, but two items in particular stand out. One is a silver salver 2 ft in diameter and richly decorated with gods and monsters surrounding a centerpiece depicting Oceanus, god of the sea. The other is a bowl with a domed lid that shows centaurs, gods, and wild animals, topped with a knob in the shape of a Triton, another sea-deity, blowing a conch-shell horn.

The presumption is that the Mildenhall Treasure was buried by a well-to-do-family to keep it from the Saxons and that, as well as being wealthy, the owners were probably well travelled because of the diverse origins of the pieces. Possibly they could have belonged to the general Lupicinus, whom the Emperor Julian sent to Britain in the 4th century to try to stem the barbarian invasions. Lupicinus was a Christian, and some of the spoons in the collection are of a type sometimes given as christening presents, although that of itself proves little. Julian, on the other hand, was the man who tried to turn the Roman Empire back to its pre-Christian beliefs. Eventually he had Lupicinus arrested, which perhaps was the reason the general never reclaimed his heirlooms.

Above:

The most spectacular hoard of Roman silver ever found in Britain was unearthed at Mildenhall in Suffolk by a farm worker, during World War II. The area, which is a rich source of Roman artifacts, was constantly threatened by Saxon raids from across the English Channel at the end of the 4th century AD, and it is assumed that the treasure was deliberately buried to conceal it from the raiders. The huge silver salver is the most striking of the 34 items in the collection, but all display exquisite craftsmanship. The treasure is now in the British Museum in London.

Emin Pasha's ivory

Above:

After months of hardship, Stanley finally reached Emin Pasha near Lake Albert in what is now Zaire. But Emin (left) was not keen to leave his hoard of ivory, and only reluctantly agreed to make for Zanzibar. Much of the ivory is still buried somewhere in the area.

For centuries, two of the most valuable commodities in Saharan and sub-Saharan Africa were black and white 'gold' — slaves and ivory respectively. Both played a part in the primitive economy of Equatoria, the area broadly corresponding to today's southern Sudan.

In 1869, the ruler of Egypt, Khedive Ismail, appointed a Briton, Samuel Baker, to annex Equatoria and to stop the slave trade there. Four years later, the bushy-bearded, piratical Baker was succeeded as governor of the province by another Briton, General Charles Gordon, known as 'Chinese' Gordon from his previous military exploits in the Far East.

An ivory hoard

The ascetic, unmarried Gordon continued Baker's fight against the slavers, and succeeded in one area in which his predecessor had failed by persuading the natives to sell their ivory only to the Egyptian government. This monopoly produced the circumstances in which one of Africa's great lost treasure mysteries was created.

Gordon rose to become governor-general of the whole of Sudan, while his place in Equatoria was taken by the German-born Emin Pasha. But by 1881, the Sudan was torn by a revolt led by the Mahdi (the name means 'divine guide'), one Mohammed Ahmed, who wanted a return to the traditional ways of Islam and to drive out all foreigners. In 1885, the Sudanese capital of Khartoum fell to the Mahdi's forces, and Gordon, who had been leading the defense, was killed.

The Mahdi's victory opened the rebels' way into Equatoria, where Emin Pasha remained with some loyal troops and about 200 tons of ivory he had collected but had been unable, because of the rebellion, to ship down the Nile. As the Mahdi's forces advanced, Emin retreated south, making caches of some of the precious elephant tusks and taking the rest with him to his new base at Wadelai.

Stanley to the rescue

Public opinion in Europe, aroused against the Mahdi by the siege of Khartoum and Gordon's death, demanded that something should be done to save Emin. In 1887, the veteran African explorer H. M. Stanley, who had previously gained fame by finding Dr David Livingstone, led a relief expedition. The expedition was beset by disasters — attacked by natives and disease, short of food, and without the promised support of 600 bearers. Eventually, Stanley and his much-depleted band reached Emin Pasha, only to find that the governor did not wish to leave.

After months of argument and cajolery, Emin was finally persuaded that he would be wiser to make for Zanzibar, on the

Left:
Stanley on his way through
Equatoria in 1887 to relieve the
beleaguered Dr Eduard Schnitzer,
better known as Mehmed Emin
Pasha, a name he adopted while
in Turkish government service.
Stanley sailed up the River Congo
and then trekked eastward
through rainforest where 200 of
his men fell prey to fever and
attacks by pygmies.

East African coast, rather than stay put. The party was too small to carry more than a fraction of the ivory Emin still had with him, so a final cache was made somewhere near Lake Albert. The border between present-day Uganda and Zaire runs down the middle of the lake.

The choice of the site was carefully calculated, for it lay in a region to which Germany had claim; Emin felt that the tusks could be reclaimed later on behalf of his native land. However, his careful planning went sadly awry, for the territory in question was eventually ceded to Britain.

Neither Emin nor Stanley ever managed to get back to the hoard. Emin was murdered in the Congo in 1892 by the very slave traders he, Gordon, and Baker had struggled against. So far as we know, he did not tell anyone of the exact location of the ivory. Stanley did not die until 1904, but he never returned to East Africa, and it is not clear whether he knew exactly where the ivory was hidden or only approximately.

Loot of the Axis

Right:

Hitler (left) shakes hands with Field Marshal Rommel during their meeting in October 1942, a turning point in the history of Germany's Third Reich. Within days, Rommel's North African troops were defeated at El Alamein, and within months Rommel was forced to flee Africa, taking with him the treasure he had accumulated.

As the Nazis invaded much of Europe in the years between 1938 and 1943, the generals looted occupied territories in a manner unprecedented in scale and organization. Public and private art galleries and museums in France, Holland, Belgium, Czechoslovakia, Poland, Hungary, and elsewhere were stripped of their glories. Churches were ransacked, and bank vaults pillaged for coin and bullion. Millions of private citizens were forced to give up jewelry, family heirlooms, and other valuables under threat of torture.

No one will ever be able to estimate the true worth of the treasures seized by the Third Reich and its allies, officially and unofficially. It certainly ran into billions of dollars, possibly trillions. Some of the works of art stolen were unique, and priceless.

Reclaiming the loot

The process of restoring this vast booty to its rightful owners began shortly after Germany surrendered in 1945, and is continuing even now. In the 1980s, for example, looted paintings were found in the home of a former Nazi official who had lived undetected for years under a false name.

According to official estimates, about 80 percent of the treasures plundered by the Nazis and their henchmen have been recovered. If one accepts that view, the value of the missing portion is still astronomical. In fact, the estimate is wildly over-optimistic; it applies only to those items known to have been stolen — that is, items of which there is some record. Millions of dollars in personal valuables alone are still missing.

Of the items officially stated to have disappeared, the bulk are either hidden or in private hands. In the chaos following the collapse of the Third Reich, many valuables were looted by private individuals of both German and occupying forces, either for themselves or for sale on the black market. As the Allied powers entered Berlin, for example, securities worth $400 million were removed from the state bank, and the fate of only a fraction of this has been satisfactorily established. At the same time, bullion, coins, and jewels worth $200 million today disappeared without trace. A joint coup by German and American soldiers is usually offered as the explanation, but no one has ever been charged with this crime.

Booty at Berchtesgaden?

Inevitably, the most persistent rumors of lost treasures from World War II attached themselves to the leaders of the Axis powers —

Hitler and the Italian dictator Benito Mussolini as well as many of the military commanders, including Field Marshal Erwin Rommel. One could fill a book with tales of Hitler's treasure which, according to preference, lies at the bottom of a mountain lake on the German-Austrian border, or in a cave or disused mine nearby, or has been removed to South America by ex-Nazis or neo-Nazis working for the resurgence of a nationalistic and militaristic Germany.

Like all theories of this type, there is probably more than a grain of truth behind them. Before his suicide in Berlin in April 1945, Hitler had been planning to continue resistance against the invading Allies from his 'final redoubt' high in the mountains of southeastern Bavaria near the picturesque town of Berchtesgaden and the Austrian city of Salzburg. Preparations for this last stand were well advanced in the spring of 1945, and it would have been natural to include in the materials destined for Berchtesgaden bullion and coin to pay loyal troops and to buy necessary armaments.

The theory is widely believed in Germany and Austria, particularly in the regions close to Berchtesgaden, where the inhabitants speak of Nazis burying large quantities of gold in the closing stages of the war. The details are blurred; the area offers several deep lakes and disused salt mines as possible hiding places, as well as large tracts of forest.

It was in the forests above Salzburg that a series of bizarre incidents occurred in the 1950s, possibly adding credibility to local rumors. In 1955, the body of a young man was found, dead from a bullet wound between the eyes. Suicide was ruled out, because the bullet did not match the gun found by the victim's body, but there were no clues as to the perpetrator or the motive. Shortly afterward, two climbers were stabbed to death nearby; close to their corpses were several holes in the ground, as though buried chests or boxes had been removed.

That would suggest that Hitler's treasure is no longer in the Salzburg/Berchtesgaden area. It may even have been smuggled to South America, the refuge of many prominent ex-Nazis. Nevertheless there are those who believe it is still somewhere near Berchtesgaden, watched over by those who consider themselves Hitler's heirs and successors.

Below:
Hitler's mountain retreat near Berchtesgaden in the Bavarian Alps was to be the command post for the Nazis' last stand against the Allies. Extensive preparations were made for defending it, but Hitler never managed to leave Berlin. However, trainloads of Nazi treasure were moved to the area in the spring of 1945, including, it is said, vast quantities of gold bullion that have never been traced.

Above and right:
Neuschwanstein Castle at Füssen,
near the Austrian frontier, was
another of the many repositories
for treasures pillaged by the Nazis
from all over Europe. When the US
7th Army uncovered the
Neuschwanstein hoard in 1945,
few of the valuable paintings had
even been removed from their
packing cases. Hitler was to have
first pick of the plunder and the
remainder was destined for the
Hermann Goering Gallery, to be
built at Linz in Austria.

Rommel's treasure

By comparison with Hitler's reputed hoard, the fate of the treasure amassed by Field Marshal Erwin Rommel, the brilliant strategist who masterminded Germany's North Africa campaign, seems relatively straightforward, although it, too, has never to public knowledge been found.

Between March 1941 and October 1942, Rommel's Afrika Korps seemed unstoppable, driving back the Allies' desert forces and gaining control over Libya, much of Tunisia, and part of northern Egypt. In his triumphant progress, Rommel collected a large amount of gold, lots of jewelry, many works of art, and ivory, destined ultimately to swell the coffers of the Third Reich.

However, the tide of battle turned at El Alamein on 23rd October 1942, and by May of the following year most of North Africa was back in Allied hands. The Afrika Korps was

forced to retreat, taking the treasure with it, and Rommel escaped back to Europe. According to most accounts, his booty was flown to the island of Corsica only a matter of days before the Allies succeeded in enforcing an air and sea blockade, and stored there under German military control.

Booty in the Gulf of Bastia

But with the Allies preparing to invade Italy, there was little prospect of getting the treasure off the island. Measures were probably taken to hide it to prevent its falling into enemy hands. At any rate, at some stage in the Fall of 1943, it disappeared. The most plausible version of events says that the spoils were taken aboard a German ship on the night of 18th September 1943, and dumped at sea in the Gulf of Bastia, at the northern corner of Corsica opposite the island of Elba. Many attempts have been made to locate it there, including one in the 1960s

involving an ex-soldier who claimed to have taken part in the dumping and therefore to know the precise spot.

He was convincing enough to persuade backers to set up a consortium and dive for the treasure. However, before the salvage operation could start, the ex-soldier suffered a sudden loss of memory and could no longer identify the location, so the expedition was called off. Shortly afterwards, the would-be guide disappeared — killed, say some, by the same ring of ex-Nazis allegedly watching over Hitler's hoard.

The mystery of Mussolini's millions

By contrast, no self-appointed band of guardians is reputedly preserving another collection of water-entrusted war spoils — the personal fortune of Italy's fascist leader, Mussolini. He was overthrown by his own people barely two months before Rommel's

treasure vanished, but escaped to the north of Italy with the aid of the Germans, who then set him up as a puppet ruler of the so-called Republic of Salò.

Early in 1945, it became clear that the Germans could no longer resist the Allied forces moving inexorably up the Italian boot. They, and Mussolini, fled. The former dictator and his mistress, Claretta Petacci, got as far as Lake Como, where they were recognized, captured, shot by partisans, and their bodies hanged upside down on public display. Otto Kisnatt, leader of Mussolini's German guards, was luckier, managing to escape and survive the war. He did so carrying two large suitcases stuffed with jewels, which he threw into Lake Como. Kisnatt kept the story to himself until 1957, when he told it to the German and Italian police. An official search was immediately organized, but neither the suitcases nor their contents have ever been found.

6

The Proceeds of Crime

Below:

Anxious clients line up in front of the closed gates of the Banque de la Société Générale in Nice, France, awaiting news of their savings. Albert Spaggiari and his accomplices had broken into the underground vaults of the bank and spent several undisturbed hours picking through the contents of safety deposit boxes.

It has been argued that those who today choose to live outside the law have never had it so good — or so easy. With modern high-tech hardware and software to aid them, ranging from computers to lasers, and plastic surgery to ultrasound, they would seem to have everything on their side. But it should be remembered that law enforcement officers also have access to these very handy helps, and they are usually better organized and better funded.

And down through the centuries the problem has not been so much one of getting hold of the loot as *getting rid* of it. Highwaymen, hijackers, outlaws, confidence tricksters and city slickers alike have all had to face this problem, and in their efforts to solve it have often left behind them sizeable caches which still await discovery. Here are some of the stories of just such proceeds of crime, and how they came to be hidden.

Underground vaults

In July 1976, an enormous haul of loot went missing from a French bank. Valued at between $8 and $10 million, it was one of the boldest, most successful, and most insolent of all bank robberies, and the proceeds are still being sought.

Ex-paratrooper and professional thief, 45-year-old Albert Spaggiari, with nine accomplices, broke into a branch of the Société Générale in Nice on 16th July. They tunneled into an underground vault, then spent 48 undisturbed hours rifling through more than 400 safety deposit boxes. While they removed jewelry, securities, bonds, and cash, they fortified themselves with food and wine they had taken in with them. Among their finds were a number of pornographic pictures which some depositor had allegedly kept there for possible blackmail purposes. The robbers grabbed these and plastered them all round the walls of the strongroom!

Early in 1977, Spaggiari was caught and brought to trial. He promised the judge that he would hand over detailed plans of how the robbery was carried out. But this magnanimous gesture *was* only a gesture. There was a brief scuffle in the courtroom and Spaggiari broke free from the guards. Using his paratroop training to good effect, he leapt out of the second-story window to land unharmed on the roof of a waiting car parked below. The car disappeared at high speed and neither the loot nor Spaggiari have been seen since.

Deadwood gold

There are numerous instances of robberies having been committed with the villains brought to trial or otherwise disposed of before all of the proceeds were recovered. As a result,

much loot still lies hidden, waiting for some lucky passer-by to stumble upon it. Just such a situation arouse from the holdup of the Deadwood Stage in 1878.

Two years before that, gold had been discovered in the Black Hills of South Dakota. Consignments were regularly transported from Deadwood, a typically lawless mining town, via the Cheyenne and Black Hills Stage Line to Cheyenne, the Wyoming capital. This particular line used an armored coach, named *Monitor*, to carry valuable cargo, and it had an enviable record of success in its operations.

An ex-soldier called Charles Carey, who had battled against Indians with Custer, cared nothing for the *Monitor*'s reputation and, tempted by the $400,000 in bullion that the stage usually carried, decided to help himself to some of it. Accordingly, on 26th September, he and his men laid an ambush at the Canyon Springs stage post, not far from Deadwood. After overpowering the stable hand and locking him in the grain store, he dispersed his band among the surrounding barns and stables.

The *Monitor* rolled into Canyon Springs on time as usual, and stopped to change its team of six horses. Carey and his men immediately opened fire, killing a telegraph operator and wounding two of the guards. But before the stage surrendered, one of the guards and the stable hand managed to escape and raise the alarm. They also slew two of Carey's gang.

Carey was then faced with the problem of opening a huge, securely locked, iron and steel chest. He knew that a posse from Deadwood would soon be at his heels, so speed was essential. Nevertheless, it took the thieves two hours to smash open the chest with sledgehammers, crowbars, and chisels. They discovered diamonds, jewelry, $3,500 in cash, and 700 lb of gold bars.

Because they had to make a quick getaway, Carey buried much of the heavy gold in two caches, one at Canyon Springs and the other at Pino Springs. It was only a matter of time before all the bandits were caught. Carey himself fell into the hands of vigilantes and was promptly hanged by them. Only a little more than half the loot was ever recovered, and the cache at Canyon Springs remains hidden to this day.

Sometimes the proceeds from a potentially huge haul are dissipated by the perpetrators in a getaway attempt. Substantial sums are paid out for safe houses, plastic surgery, false passports, and the like, and at the end of it all, the miserable fugitive is lucky if he can survive without having to work for a living once more. Money disappeared fast in this way after what was billed as the crime of the century in England: the Great Train Robbery.

Above:
In this raid on a branch of the American Security and Trust Company in Washington, DC, three armed men burst into the building while a fourth man waited in a car outside. In the background one of the robbers holds his gun to the head of a guard; a second man aims his gun at the staff; and a third clambers over the counter to get at the money. In spite of all three being caught on film by the bank's hidden camera, the robbers got away with more than $10,000.

The Great Train Robbery

It took place in 1963, on the evening of 7th August. The Royal Mail Train (in reality a travelling post office) left Glasgow, Scotland, on its way to Euston Station in London, where it was scheduled to arrive the following morning. Right at the front of the train was a special van holding 120 bags. Each bag was stuffed with used and grubby bills. At 3 o'clock in the morning, about 36 miles from London, on a lonely stretch of track, the driver stopped for a red signal.

Masked men, armed with iron bars, axes, and other weapons, suddenly rushed the train and overpowered the driver and guard. They uncoupled the locomotive and the van with the money in it, leaving the rest of the train stationary on the track, with the postal sorters busily working and blissfully unaware of what had happened. They broke into the high-value van after pulling it half a mile down the track to where a convenient bridge carried the getaway cars and trucks.

The workers inside the van quickly surrendered when faced with the masked gang, and within half an hour $4.2 million (£2.6 million) had been transferred to a temporary hideout. This was a recently rented farmhouse, Leatherslade Farm, in deserted countryside near Oakley, in Buckinghamshire. It was some 18 miles from the scene of the holdup.

There were allegedly 17 robbers in all. If so, three of them have never been traced. Seven men were the big fish. They had planned everything in meticulous detail, including faking the signals to stop the train originally and cutting the emergency telephone wires by the track. But when the seven came to divide the spoils in the farmhouse, they grew careless and left fingerprints all over the place.

In spite of the fact that the crooks had at least an hour's start, the police were soon on their trail. The seven were all eventually rounded up, tried, convicted, and sentenced to an astonishing term (in England) of 30 years each in jail. This was later reduced on appeal.

Below:
The so-called British Great Train Robbery of 1963 is the largest recorded train robbery of all time. The bandits got away with 120 mailbags stuffed with about £2,632,000 ($4.2 million) in used bills. Nearly all the robbers were eventually caught, but only £343,448 ($580,000) was ever recovered. The picture shows a man of average height standing beside the mountainous stack of bills that would have made up the huge haul.

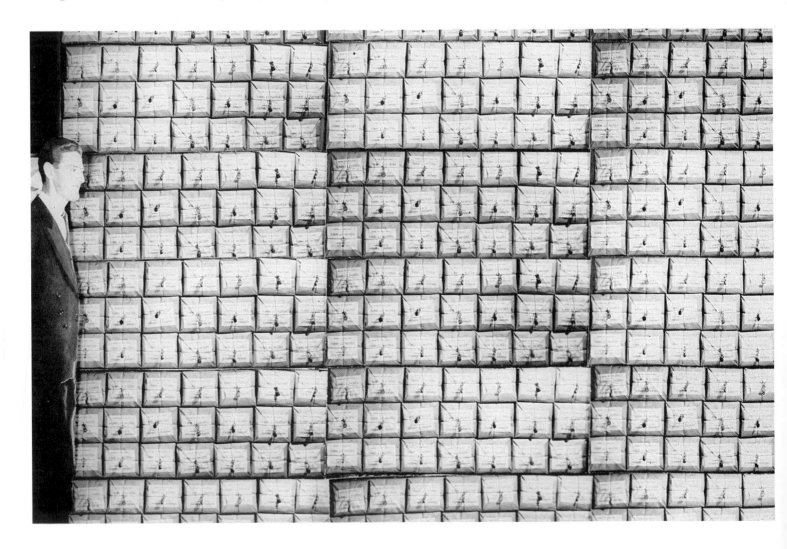

Each of the top men took about $270,000 out of the kitty. As the police closed in, some of the robbers began to lose their nerve and looked for places to hide the cash that weighed so heavily on them. Some $34,000 was found in a little Surrey town called East Molesey. A car and a truck in London concealed another $190,000. A similar sum turned up in a forest near Dorking, and $54,000 was discovered in an abandoned caravan.

Only two men managed to hold on to their share of the loot. Douglas Gordon Goody salted his $270,000 away so well that it presumably awaited him after he had served his time. Ronald Arthur Biggs, the most notorious of the gang, escaped from jail after 12 months. He fled first to Australia and then to Rio, where, in the mid-1980s, he was still living. But all his money had been spent in high-priced bribes to ensure his safe flight halfway across the world. In Brazil he lived in spartan surroundings and was reduced to simple carpentering jobs and expensive interviews in order to make ends meet.

As for the rest of the haul? Well, about $4 million is still missing, perhaps scattered somewhere along the green and leafy lanes of Buckinghamshire.

US find

Sometimes the proceeds of a criminal haul can never be recovered. Such a situation arose after the theft of the crown jewels of Hesse-Darmstadt, one of the great old aristocratic families of Europe.

Toward the end of World War II, the Grand Duchess Margarethe of Hesse moved out of her home, Kronberg Castle, in the Taunus Mountains, in Germany, and gave it up to General Patton's advancing armies. But before she did so, she hid the family jewels under a stone slab in the cellar of the castle, for safe keeping until after the war.

During her absence the box was found by some American soldiers, forced open, and apparently handed over to some officers. Early in 1946, Princess Sophie of Hesse was about to get married to Prince Georg Wilhelm of Hanover. She decided she would like to wear some of the jewels (family heirlooms) at her wedding, so she went to the Americans who were still occupying the castle and asked them to return the jewels.

This was the first the Americans had heard

Left:
Great Train Robber Ronald Biggs, the one who got away, in sunny Rio de Janeiro with his son, Mike, whose birth saved him by Brazilian law from deportation to Britain. Allegedly most of Bigg's share of the loot was spent on making his escape from an English prison.

of the affair. Subsequent inquiries showed that among the residents of the castle at the time that the jewels went missing was a welfare officer, Captain Kathleen B. Nash, and a Colonel James W. Durant. These two had married soon after their return to the States. During a routine check by investigators, the Durants began to run. They were arrested, and eventually the true story came out.

The soldiers who found the jewels apparently took them to Miss Nash, who then showed them to Durant. The two of them, together with a Major Watson, decided to take the jewels, sell them, and start a business on the proceeds.

After questioning, Durant took his interrogators to a rented locker in the Chicago station of the Illinois Central Railroad. There, in a cardboard box, lay a heap of gleaming jewels, carefully prised from their costly settings. More of the Hesse-Darmstadt regalia was found at the home of Mrs Durant's sister, who had accepted as a gift a solid gold dinner service studded with gems. Unaware of its value and historic associations, she had kept it for everyday use! Up to that time, the investigators had recovered about half $500,000 worth of the treasure.

Above:
During a robbery at the Lee-Harvard branch of the National City Bank in Cleveland, Ohio, one of the gunmen noticed the camera and pumped it full of lead. Nevertheless, pictures taken by the camera led to one arrest and the identification of a suspect.

Bracelets and tiaras

Major David F. Watson was the next to be located, still serving in Germany. After spending some time with him, the investigators were able to lay their hands on more of the loot: diamond bracelets, pearl tiaras, and amethyst rings. Some of the original settings also turned up in a goldsmith's shop in Belfast, Northern Ireland.

All these items were proudly returned to the Grand Duchess in Frankfurt, but she was adamant that many items were still missing. While the army agents resumed their search, Mrs Durant was tried, found guilty of theft, and sentenced to five years in jail and dishonorable discharge from the army. Watson was also found guilty, and was given three years and a dishonorable discharge. Durant, the alleged mastermind behind the conspiracy, was sentenced to 15 years' hard labor and was dismissed from the army.

Shortly before Durant's trial, three quart pickle jars had been found buried by a roadside in Durant's home state of Virginia. Two contained jewels wrenched from the Hesse regalia, and the third was stuffed with cash to the tune of some $15,000. Later, more jewels were discovered in the walls of a cottage in the grounds of Kronberg Castle.

And that was just about the final tally. Much of the regalia, according to Prince Philip of Hesse, is still missing and unaccounted for. It will probably never be recovered because the missing gems will no doubt have been cut and reshaped to make them unidentifiable and saleable on the international market.

Colonel Blood

Another crown jewel robbery ended on a happier note. This involved the English crown jewels and took place centuries ago. The jewels were originally stolen by Oliver Cromwell in 1649. They were then recovered and returned to the Tower of London under heavy guard. In an apartment above the jewel room in Martin Tower (part of the Tower of London), there lived a man and wife called Talbot and Dolly Edwardes whose job was to clean the jewels and help guard them. They also acted as guides, greeting distinguished visitors who had permission to view the jewels and giving a running commentary.

In April 1671, the Edwardes were visited by a clergyman and his wife. They paid several visits to the Tower and eventually struck up a social friendship with the Edwardes. On one of these visits the minister confided that he was acquainted with a rich young man who would make an ideal match for the Edwardes' daughter, and he arranged to bring the gentleman with him on his next visit so that the prospective parents-in-law could give him the once-over.

Left:
A bank raid in London, England in 1981, filmed by a hidden TV camera. After £4,000 ($7,000) in cash was handed over by helpless staff, one of the three armed youths involved in the robbery incautiously pulled down his face mask, thus providing the police with an excellent mugshot.

A royal reprieve

On 9th May, the clergyman returned with not one but two men, one he called his nephew, and the other the alleged suitor. The minister suggested that Edwardes might care to show his friends round the jewel room. Edwardes complied, but as soon as they entered the room, the three men knocked him down, and bound and gagged him. They then set about taking the jewels.

The minister flattened the crown with a mallet, in order to slip it into his pocket. The second man grabbed hold of the golden ball of the royal orb. The third man filed the scepter in half and put one half in each of two specially made pockets. As they were leaving the Tower, the guards spotted them and raised the alarm. Within an hour the treasure had been recovered and the thieves apprehended.

The fake parson turned out to be the notorious Colonel Thomas Blood, an Irish rebel who had fought Cromwell and who had already attempted several times to kidnap the English royal family. At his trial, Blood refused to answer questions unless they were put to him directly by the king himself. Charles II was so intrigued by this effrontery that he insisted on making a personal visit to the prisoner. During the ensuing conversation, the monarch was so impressed and amused that he reprieved Blood from his mandatory death sentence. He also restored his estate and granted him an annual pension of £300, a princely sum in those days.

Colonel Blood was no doubt grateful for large mercies but saw no reason to change his ways. He continued to plot against the Crown until his death in 1680.

Capone's concrete 'cashbox'

Above:
Al Capone (1899-1947) was undisputed king of America's underworld during the 1920s and 1930s. After a knife brawl that left him with an angry scar running from eye to lip, he became known as 'Scarface'. With his headquarters in Chicago, he climbed to the top in crime by eliminating rivals through intimidation, bribery, and murder. After a seemingly charmed career of unremitting violence, he was finally jailed for tax offenses, and eventually died in obscurity of tertiary syphilis.

In the mid-1980s, workers demolishing an abandoned ten-story building were astonished to uncover a mysterious concrete vault which is believed to have been built on the orders of Al Capone. There was excited speculation about its contents, ranging from bodies, booze, and a car, to substantial amounts of his ill-gotten and still missing gains, in cash, or gold, or both.

Al Capone was the infamous gangster who became a worldwide symbol of Prohibition crime in the 1920s and 1930s. He built up an enormous and much-feared organization that had its fingers in many criminal pies, including bribery, prostitution, gambling, and illegal liquor sales. He organized the notorious St Valentine's Day massacre of 1929 when some of his gang mowed down eight rival gangsters with machine-guns. In spite of his murderous record, and a personal fortune built up from robbery and extortion that was estimated at more than $1000 million, all the police could indict him for was income tax evasion. For this he was fined $70,000 and jailed for 11 years in 1931. In 1939, he was released from Alcatraz, and survived semi-paralyzed until 1947.

The building where the vault was found was known to be Capone's Chicago headquarters during his heyday. The vault was located beneath the sidewalk in front of the old Lexington Hotel (a 400-room brothel in Capone's era) on Michigan Avenue. The vault itself is 125 ft long, 6 ft high, and 6 ft wide.

Fascinating sidelights arose from renewed interest in the old gangster's elaborate hideaway. Chicago's central business district is apparently honeycombed with underground railroad tunnels. Originally they were used to facilitate the movement of coal to downtown stores and offices. Later, they housed steam pipes, and today fiber-optic cables have been laid along their length.

It appears that in the 1930s Capone employed an army of Italian immigrants to dig tunnels to link his headquarters with these railroad tunnels. As a result, he had access to most key city offices, including City Hall. The tunnels also provided handy escape routes in emergencies, and were used to carry consignments of bootleg liquor to various parts of the city. The hotel itself was riddled with secret exits, and Capone once boasted that he could completely empty the hotel within a quarter of an hour without anybody ever having to use the streets. Capone reserved one entire floor for himself and ensconced his mistress comfortably on the floor above.

Rumors of vast wealth cached away somewhere in the building have persisted over the years since the gangster's death. Sewer workers have reported finding jewelry in the drains, including a diamond-and-sapphire stickpin and several gold coins. But when the vault was finally opened, in front of TV cameras and amid wide publicity, it proved a huge disappointment. There was nothing inside of value — and certainly nothing to justify the $800,000 lien slapped on the putative contents by the Internal Revenue Service, still pursuing tax claims against Capone's estate. So if the rumors of Scarface's treasure are true, it must lie elsewhere in the labyrinth beneath downtown Chicago.

Above:

Federal agents proudly uncover a bootlegger's illicit liquor still during the Prohibition era, before pouring away its contents into the sewers. By the late 1920s, Al Capone had established a bootlegging empire that netted more than $1000 million a year in profits. He got rid of all competition by corrupting the police, rigging elections, and murdering those who did not cooperate. Bootleg liquor, however, had quite nasty side effects — it contained poisons that could blind, paralyze, or kill — earning the nicknames 'rotgut' and 'coffin varnish'.

Big hoard on the Big Horn

Almost everybody has heard of Custer's Last Stand in the Battle of the Little Big Horn. What many people don't realize is that at the time of the massacre, and in roughly the same area, a whole heap of gold went missing, and is still being sought today. The strange cycle of events was unearthed by American author Emile C. Schumacher during some research into military history.

Crazy Horse

Three strands came together on that fateful day in 1876, June 25th. The first consisted of Lieutenant-Colonel George Armstrong Custer himself, commanding the 7th Cavalry. He and his regiment were seeking to capture escaped Sioux and Cheyenne Indians in order to return them to their reservations. Custer was in Montana Territory in a region bounded by the Big Horn, Little Big Horn, and Little Horn rivers. He came across an Indian camp in a valley along the Little Big Horn River. Believing that the camp held only about 1,000 Indians, and disdaining the offer of help and reinforcements from Brigadier-General Alfred Terry to the east, Custer hurled his force of 225 tired men into the attack. The camp contained at least 1,500 fighting men (some reports put the figure as high as 5,000) led by such legendary characters as Sitting Bull, Crazy Horse, and Gall. Within an hour, Custer's column was wiped out to a man.

The second strand in the saga was the riverboat *Far West*, hired by the US Cavalry to supply the troops with food and equipment. The *Far West*, skippered by 52-year-old Grant Marsh, drew less than 2 ft of water in ballast, and was ideal for navigating shallow unknown waters. At the time of Custer's ill-timed foray, the riverboat was plying the Big Horn en route to a rendezvous with General Terry at the junction of the Big Horn and the Little Big Horn rivers.

The third strand involved a mule-drawn freight wagon galloping along a dusty trail some 50 miles west of the Big Horn River. It had set out from Bozeman, Montana, and was headed for Bismark, North Dakota. On board were the driver, Gil Longworth, two men riding shotgun, Jergens and Dickson, and a shipment

Right:
'Custer's Last Stand' has been immortalized and mythologized in story, song, poetry, and painting, as in this romantic lithography by Otto Becker. The harsh truth of the matter is that General George Custer deliberately disobeyed a military order. He and his 225 men paid the penalty with their lives.

of miners' gold in dust and nuggets valued at about $50,000. Longworth and his two guards were distinctly unhappy. They had already survived a couple of attacks by marauding Indians and the remainder of the journey was fraught with danger.

Meanwhile, the *Far West* had missed the agreed rendezvous with General Terry by sailing past the confluence of the two rivers. Marsh was preparing to return downstream when he spotted Longworth and his wagon on the river bank. Longworth begged Marsh to relieve him of the gold because the area was crawling with hostile Indians. Marsh agreed, and the gold was hastily shipped aboard the *Far West*.

Later that evening, Marsh became aware of increasing Indian activity all around him and decided it would be prudent to hide the gold somewhere ashore and collect it later. Accordingly, Marsh himself, Foulk (his engineer) and Ben Thompson (his first mate) warily rowed ashore with the bags of gold and buried them.

Bullet-ridden

By this time Terry had joined battle with the Sioux and driven them off, only to discover the corpses of Custer and his men. He finally rendezvoused with the *Far West* and commandeered the boat to ferry his wounded troops to Bismark. Marsh was therefore unable

to retrieve the gold. Gil Longworth failed to run the Indian gauntlet and his bullet-ridden body was discovered some days later.

In 1879, Marsh tried to trace Longworth's employers and the names of the owners of the gold, which had been sewn onto tabs on individual bags. But it was all in vain. Marsh, Thompson, and Foulk, the three men who knew exactly where the treasure was hidden, went on working for the rest of their lives with no signs of having acquired sudden significant wealth. The assumption must be, therefore, that the gold still lies where it was cached in 1876. It is known that the site lies some 15 to 20 miles up the Big Horn River from its junction with the Little Big Horn, on the west bank.

Pie in the sky

Above:

The audacious skyjacker who leaped out of a Northwest Airlines Boeing 727 in 1971, hugging a $200,000 ransom to his body, disappeared literally out of the blue. He called himself 'D. B. Cooper'. An artist's composite picture, released by the FBI and based on a description by fellow passengers, shows him as a swarthy middle-aged man with dark glasses.

Far right:

'D. B. Cooper' was unquestionably an experienced parachutist who knew what he was doing. In spite of being denied all the safety equipment he had demanded, and unlooked-for complications with the cash holdall, he timed his jump precisely. Some experts believe that he may have landed in a tiny wooded area east of Washington.

On 24th November 1971 a man leapt out of an airplane over the state of Washington clutching $200,000, and neither hide nor hair of him or the money has been seen since.

The story of the first skyjacker to parachute to earth with his loot (since dubbed 'parajacker') began when a man who gave his name as D. B. Cooper boarded a Boeing 727 at Portland, Oregon. With hindsight, it is obvious that he was a skilled parachutist who chose his aircraft well. The Boeing 727 has a tail-exit which would allow a jumper to keep clear of fuselage and engines.

Described as a tall, powerfully built man in his mid-forties, Cooper was wearing a black trenchcoat over a conventional outfit of coat and slacks. He hid only behind brown-tinted glasses, sat at the back of the plane, and spoke and acted quietly. During the flight he asked the air hostess to pass a note to the pilot in which he demanded $200,000 in $20 bills stacked in a knapsack, plus two backpack and two chestpack parachutes. To encourage the hostess, he opened his briefcase and showed her what looked like a number

of sticks of dynamite wired together.

This was all to take place after the aircraft had made its first stop at Seattle. Refueling there was deliberately slowed down, and for the first time Cooper noticeably began to lose his cool. Nor was he too pleased when the money he had demanded was brought to him in a white cloth sack. This meant that he would have to carry it instead of being able to sling it from his shoulders. The 10,000 $20 bills weighed a manageable 24 lb, packed into a parcel measuring just 8 x 6 x 27 inches — further evidence of Cooper's careful planning.

After taking off from Seattle, Cooper ordered pilot W. Bill Scott to head for Mexico City via Reno, Nevada. He was given very precise instructions. He was to fly at a steady height of 7,000 ft, let down the landing gear, and use 15 percent flaps. This meant that the aircraft would be flying through the night at around 200 mph, thus enabling Cooper to calculate his position over a predetermined dropping zone with reasonable accuracy.

Soon after take-off Cooper ordered the rear exit from the plane to be opened, and 32 minutes after departure from Seattle, at 20:13 precisely, he baled out. He left two of the parachutes behind him on the aircraft. One had strips torn off it — these were presumably used to bind the money sack to his body. He jumped with just one serviceable backpack, because the other chestpack he took with him was intended for ground practice only, and was useless in the air.

There ensued an almost immediate and intensive search for the missing skyjacker and his loot. His landing zone, calculated by computer, seems to have been an area of about 15 square miles some 30 to 40 miles north of Portland. Right there, Cooper would have landed in heavily wooded country at the foot of the Cascade Mountains.

Public reaction to the exploit was often one of admiration. A devoted parajack cult built up on the West Coast, and graphic T-shirts inscribed 'D. B. Cooper — Where Are You?' sold out rapidly. Seven years later, a deerhunter in the Oregon woods came across an interior warning sign from the door of a Boeing 727. The discovery brought new hordes of treasure seekers to the area, and one of

them stumbled on $3,000 in notes, identifiable as part of the loot by the serial numbers, scattered near a river bank. But of the rest of there was no sign. Perhaps Cooper lies rotting somewhere with $197,000 beside him.

7

Art Mysteries

The problem with works of art, unlike many of the treasures described in this book, is that their value depends entirely on their cultural significance as 'art'. Unlike, say, a hoard of gold coins or precious stones, they have no intrinsic value. As such, they have attracted the attention of the acquisitive down the ages, but for an unusual variety of reasons, and often with curiously double-edged results.

The appreciation of art as worthwhile treasure is largely the product of the enlightened attitude of the Renaissance. In Roman times, conquering generals were expected to bring home large quantities of loot from their vanquished enemies, their success being judged by the number of slaves they captured or by the chests of gold coins they plundered, but these were largely practical benefits in the timeless tradition of sack and pillage. The slaves were a useful addition to the workforce, and the gold offset the cost of training, feeding, equipping, and paying an army. Articles of artistic merit were of no significance unless they had a strictly financial value.

Nothing typifies this philistine attitude more than the activities of the conquistadores in the New World in the 15th century; many of the items they plundered from the Aztec and Inca empires were of extraordinary beauty, but this did not interest the Spaniards in the slightest. Everything made of precious metal was melted down and converted to bankable bullion and spendable coin. With the coming of the Renaissance, however, art and learning were appreciated for their own sake, and it became fashionable for cultured princes to surround themselves with works of art. The very fact that works of art were appreciated for their own sake, however, gave them a financial value; as soon as demand goes up, so does the price. In the late 18th and early 19th centuries there was a positive mania for collecting art treasures from across the world. Collectors felt a certain righteousness in 'rescuing' them from oblivion and neglect.

In 1803, Britain's Lord Elgin loaded the famous Elgin Marbles onto a boat and packed them off to his Scottish castle. The marbles were the frieze of the Parthenon in Athens, and Elgin's motives were not entirely selfish, for the Parthenon had suffered terribly under years of Turkish rule and its treasures were in danger of being completely ruined. Elgin simply felt that Britain was a safer place for them than Greece. Unfortunately, the sight of his workmen attacking the ancient ruins with hammer and

chisel offended contemporary sensibilities and Elgin received little but criticism for his pains. He eventually tried to sell his collection to the British Museum for £74,240 ($125,000), a sum he calculated would scarcely cover his expenses. He was forced to settle, in the end, for £35,000 ($60,000) and a good deal of disillusion. A new museum is now being built in Athens to house *all* the objects from the Parthenon. Will the Elgin Marbles finally be returned to their place of origin?

Napoleonic plunder

And yet Elgin's actions were as nothing compared to one of his contemporaries.

Napoleon Bonaparte was, quite shamelessly, one of the greatest looters of art treasures in history, not for financial gain, either personally or nationally, but for the cultural glory of France. He believed that France was rightly the artistic center of the world and that, by virtue of her political strength, she was entitled to house and protect all the great treasures of Europe. With extraordinary arrogance, he proclaimed: 'All men of genius are French, no matter in what country they happen to have been born.' To that end, he appointed an aristocrat of great energy and discerning taste, Baron Dominique Vivant Denon, to mastermind his campaign of acquisition.

Above:

Even if the Elgin Marbles are one day returned to Greece, they will not be replaced on the Parthenon itself, which is being eroded by pollution. Besides, part of the supporting structure was destroyed during their rather brutal removal by Lord Elgin during his term as British Ambassador to Turkey.

Above:
Shortly before the fighting began
at the abbey of Monte Cassino, the
Germans evacuated the monks.
The monastery's priceless
collection of art treasures was
packed up and removed 'for safe
keeping', although several items
disappeared en route and have
never been seen again.

Denon shared Bonaparte's ideals and lack of scruples. He began his work in Egypt, taking not only treasures but invaluable information from the tombs of the pharaohs, sometimes working under fire as the French troops overran the country. With Napoleon's successful campaign in Italy, even greater opportunities presented themselves. In December 1797, he even took the great bronze horses of San Marco from outside the basilica in Venice. The people of Venice were so incensed and outraged that they rioted in the streets, and French troops had to keep them back at bayonet point. But away the horses went, to be paraded in triumph around the Champ de Mars in Paris with other examples of cultural booty. The Louvre — originally called the Musée Napoléon — was given to Denon to house the outstanding collection. Napoleon's regime did not last very long, however, and when it collapsed the European allies soon arrived to collect their lost property. To the disgust of Denon and the impotent anger of

many of his colleagues, over 2,000 paintings and hundreds of sculptures, engravings, and objets d'art were repatriated, including the horses of San Marco.

Hitler's hauls

A century later, Adolf Hitler had precisely the same idea. A skilled, if unimaginative, painter and architect himself, Hitler dreamed of fulfilling his frustrated artistic leanings by creating a collection that would remain a permanent testimony to the achievement of his Reich. He grew up in the town of Linz, in Austria, and had fond memories of it, so he made Linz the object of his obsession. He planned to have the whole town rebuilt in the portentous approved Nazi style, arranged around a hugh showpiece gallery. 'Sonderauftrag Linz' (Special Operation Linz) set out to glean works of art from every country invaded by the forces of the Third Reich — with the possible exception of Russia, whose ancient artistic tradition

Left:
Some paintings seem to attract the special attention of art thieves. Rembrandt's portrait of Jacob de Gheyn III is one of the world's most stolen pictures. It was stolen from a London gallery in 1966, 1973, and 1981; each time it was recovered. In 1983, however, it was stolen again and has not reappeared.

Hitler despised on racial grounds.

In conquered countries, art treasures were simply confiscated. In allied countries, a modicum of protocol was observed. Many of Italy's art treasures had been taken to the mountaintop refuge of Monte Cassino monastery; when fighting threatened the monastery, German soldiers offered to evacuate the treasures to a safe place. Most were taken under guard to the Vatican, but a few were mislaid on the journey and found their way to Germany. Vichy France undertook to look after Belgium's priceless Van Eyck altarpiece from Ghent Cathedral, but the Germans traced it and took it away anyway. Treasures belonging to murdered Jews were taken over by the state,

and many a minor Nazi official, seeking to curry favor, acquired a picture or a statue and presented it to the Fuehrer. At the end of the war, thousands of objects intended for Linz were found in an Austrian salt mine. And Hitler's chief lieutenant, Hermann Goering, a man of more flamboyant tastes and keener discernment than Hitler, went into business on his own account, amassing a superb collection of paintings and sculptures at his Karinhall villa. With the fall of the Nazis in 1945, the Allies were faced with the tremendous headache of trying to return such works of art to their rightful owners. The work is still going on today. Many items were lost or mislaid simply because of the anarchic state of Europe

Above:
The beautiful medieval crown of Saint Stephen, part of the coronation regalia of the Hungarian monarchy, was seized by Hungarian fascists at the end of World War II to prevent it from falling into the hands of the Russians. It was then handed over to the Americans, who kept it for many years before handing it back in 1978.

Far right:
The motives of art thieves vary. Many, of course, are just in it for the money, but others steal paintings to publicize themselves or their particular aims. This picture, Vermeer's 'Girl with a Guitar', was stolen in 1974 to support the cause of the IRA. Despite threats that it would be destroyed on St Patrick's night, it was returned largely undamaged.

in the aftermath of hostilities. The Hungarian Crown of St Stephen, for example, a medieval crown with great symbolic significance, was stolen by Hungarian fascists to prevent it falling into the hands of the advancing Russians. It was handed over to the Americans for safe keeping and kept in Fort Knox for many years, until President Carter had it returned to the Hungarian people in 1978.

A catalog of crimes

Most art thieves lack the extraordinary resources of a Hitler or a Napoleon. And yet they, too, have obsessional motives. The most famous art theft of all, Vincenzo Perugia's 1911 attempt on the 'Mona Lisa', was prompted by a desire to restore a great work of art to his native Italy, a belated compensation for the ravages of Napoleon. In 1939, Serge-Claus Bogousslavsky stole Watteau's 'L'Indifférent' from the Louvre because, he said, he loved Watteau and the painting had been badly treated and needed loving restoration. A jury decided that Bogousslavsky's high ideals had, in fact, damaged the painting and sent him to prison for four years. In 1958, two small Van Dycks, then worth about $14,000, disappeared from a gallery in Aix-en-Provence in France. Three days later, they were found on a window ledge with a note explaining that they had been taken as a bet. In 1974, Vermeer's 'Girl

with a Guitar' was stolen from Kenwood House in London by Irish nationalists, who demanded that the sisters Dolours and Marion Price, in prison in Britain for terrorist crimes, should be returned to their native Northern Ireland. Despite threats that the picture would be burned on St Patrick's night, it was eventually found abandoned in a London churchyard.

A popular theory is that behind many art crimes is an eccentric collector, keen to own his favorite paintings whatever the cost and lock them away in a secret vault where only he may see them. Such a scenario is by no means impossible — remember Goering. In December 1983, one of the world's largest art thefts occurred at Mexico's National Anthropology Museum. The robbers took 140 priceless gold, jade, and obsidian artifacts, including some of the famous Mayan artifacts from the well at Chichén Itzá. Since the trade in pre-Columbian treasures has a shady element to it, it is possible that these items may have ended up in private collections. Certainly they were all too well known to be sold publicly. Similarly, the paintings stolen from the Marmottan Museum in Paris are of value only for ransom or to a collector, and the same can be said of those stolen by thieves posing as policemen from a Boston (US) gallery in March 1990. The works in that haul, including Rembrandt's 'Storm on the Sea of Galilee', were valued at around $300 million, making it the biggest art theft in history. By far the most usual motive for art theft is the hope of a quick profit. Many small treasures are stolen from private collections and sold to unsuspecting dealers. In the case of more valuable pieces, their fame counts against them, for they are often too hot to sell. As the gang that robbed several wealthy galleries on the French Riviera in the 1960s discovered, the only hope is usually to ransom them back to the owners, often at a fraction of the value.

And yet art crime seems to be growing. Interpol, which tries to keep a central record of stolen works of art, has up to 70,000 cases on its books at any one time. Some pieces seem to suffer more than others. Rembrandt's portrait of Jacob de Gheyn III is one of the world's most stolen masterpieces. It was taken from London's Dulwich Picture Gallery in 1966, recovered, stolen again in 1973, and again in 1981. In 1983, thieves broke in through a skylight and took it again. It has yet to be found.

Theft of the Mona Lisa

The half smile on the lips of Leonardo da Vinci's famous portrait of the 'Mona Lisa' is justifiably renowned, and many have wondered as to its significance. On at least one occasion, this most famous of painted ladies had cause to look mysterious for, as a Paris paper commented at the time, she had 'eloped' and caused quite a stir.

Leonardo painted his masterpiece in Florence between 1503 and 1506, his subject being Mona Lisa, second wife of Zanobi del Giocondo — sometimes called 'La Gioconda'. It was clearly a picture Leonardo valued himself, for when he emigrated to France he took it with him. It was eventually sold to Francis I for 4,000 gold coins. It hung in the royal palaces of Fontainebleau or Versailles, and may have adorned Napoleon's bedroom at the Tuileries. In 1804, it was presented to the Louvre gallery in Paris.

One day in 1911, a maintenance man noticed that the 'Mona Lisa' was missing from her usual place on the wall. He joked to his colleagues that it had been removed to prevent his stealing it, but they did not suspect anything wrong. The painting was frequently removed to be photographed, copied, or engraved. The next morning, Brigadier Poupardin of the Louvre guards also noticed that it was missing, but thought that it had been taken for photographing. About 9 o'clock in the morning, a painter, Louis Béroud, who was completing a picture of the gallery which housed the masterpiece, asked where it was. He was told that the photographer was copying it. When it had not been returned by midday, he insisted that Brigadier Poupardin investigate. The red-faced guard commander returned with the breathtaking news that the picture was nowhere to be found.

The world reacts

When the news reached the press that afternoon, it was greeted with incredulity. One paper ran the story under the simple headline *Inimaginable!* To the Parisian public, deeply in love with their national art treasures, it was a monstrous crime. Many simply refused to believe it. It was all a hoax, they said, to prove the painting's vulnerability, to embarrass some official, or to sell more newspapers. The prefect of police was called in and began a systematic search of the Louvre. When it was opened in 1793, France's foremost gallery had contained a mere 155 objects, but now it covered 49 acres, housed over 500,000 items, and contained a maze of underground storage chambers. The magazine *L'Illustration* offered a reward of 40,000 francs for the return of the painting, no questions asked. *Paris-Journal* topped this with an offer of 50,000 francs. The police managed to piece together the crime.

The thief had probably hidden in the building overnight and, before too many guards were about, had simply unhooked the

picture from the wall. He then went into a store-room, stripped the binding from the back of the frame, and took the picture out, leaving the frame behind. He then unscrewed a bolt to get through a door. A plumber whom he bumped into in the corridor assumed he was a fellow workman who was lost and showed him out of the building.

For several months, Paris was in uproar. Everyone had theories about the crime. Some thought that the painting had been stolen by an art student in love with the face; others that it had been destroyed by a lunatic. Psychics pronounced on its fate. Mysterious strangers were questioned, rumors abounded. So

did recriminations — the Louvre's curator, Théophile Homolle, was sacked, and security at the gallery was tightened.

There was an interesting diversion involving the poet Guillaume Apollinaire and his friend Pablo Picasso. Some years earlier, it transpired, Apollinaire had been offered two statues stolen from the Louvre by an eccentric named Géry Pieret. He had refused them, but Picasso had bought them. In the aftermath of the 'Mona Lisa' robbery, Pieret confessed to another statue theft, and Picasso and Apollinaire, in panic, tried to return the first two to a newspaper. Apollinaire was arrested and interrogated about the theft of the 'Mona

Below:

One of the greatest artists of the 20th century, Pablo Picasso, pictured with his wife in 1919, several years after the 'Mona Lisa' scandal. Picasso and his friend Apollinaire, who had been offered other items stolen from the Louvre, were both questioned over the Leonardo theft.

Probably the most famous painting in the world, Leonardo du Vinci's 'Mona Lisa', abducted from the Louvre in 1911. The motives of the thief still arouse speculation, and it has been suggested that, during its absence from the Louvre, the painting was copied and the copies sold off as the original to unscrupulous American collectors.

Lisa' itself. Happily, he was innocent, and the police rather reluctantly released him.

The finding

It was two years before the masterpiece turned up. One day in November 1913, an Italian art dealer, Alfredo Geri, received a note from Paris offering him the 'Mona Lisa'. At first he was inclined to treat it as a joke, but on second thoughts he showed it to his friend Giovanni Poggi, the curator of the Uffizi gallery. They decided to arrange a meeting with the writer of the letter, who turned out to be a tall, thin young man named Vincenzo Perugia. Perugia led them back to his lodgings, took a parcel from under his bed, and unwrapped the missing masterpiece.

The finding of the 'Mona Lisa' caused almost as much of a sensation as its theft. In the Italian Chamber of Deputies a fist fight between political rivals broke up when the news was announced. Perugia, pressed for a motive, declared he had stolen it (by posing as a workman to enter the Louvre) to redress Napoleon's looting of Italian art treasures — although cynics pointed out that Perugia had asked Geri for 500,000 lire for its return. He was tried, found guilty, and sentenced to one year and 15 days' imprisonment, although, on appeal, he was released after seven months. The painting itself went on a tour of Italy, where it drew rapturous crowds, particularly in Florence, before being returned to the embarrassed officials in France.

It is impossible to estimate the value of such a painting. It was not, and never would be, for sale. However, The *New York Times* wryly pointed out that if Francis I had bought it for 400 gold pieces in 1506, its value in 1913, at 3 percent compound interest, would have been in the region of $1,629,528.062. And interest on that sum would mount up at the rate of $94.30 a minute!

The strange case of the disappearing Duke

Above:
Experts study the Goya masterpiece after its return to London's National Gallery in May 1965. The Duke was lucky; there was some minor damage, but basically the picture was in good condition. Not all stolen works of art are treated with such consideration.

On 21st August 1961, London's National Gallery in Trafalgar Square had an averagely busy day — some 5,690 visitors passed through its doors. One, at least, left in a highly unorthodox fashion, climbing out through a back bathroom window. With him he took Goya's portrait 'The Duke of Wellington'.

Initial police investigations drew a blank, but 10 days later the news agency Reuters received an anonymous note, written in plain capitals and bearing a London postmark. After carefully describing notes and stretching devices on the back of the frame, which only the thief would know, it went on to say: 'The picture is not, and will not be for sale — it is for ransom — £140,000, to be given to charity. If a fund is started, it should be quickly made up, and on the promise of a free pardon for the culprits, the picture will be handed back... All good people are urged to give, and help the affair to a speedy conclusion.'

Ransom demands for stolen works of art are no rarity but seldom has one claimed such a Robin Hood motive — stealing from the rich to give to the poor! If the note was intended to attract publicity, it certainly succeeded. The influential London *Times*, intrigued, ran a piece which likened the thief to the fictional gentleman cracksman Raffles, famed for his ability to steal the unstealable. Perhaps, suggested *The Times*, the thief might like to test his skill by returning the picture to a major Goya exhibition without being caught? The thief was not tempted, and a large reward offered by the gallery had no luck either.

More offers

As time went by, the missing Goya became a *cause célèbre*, the intrigue surrounding it being expressed by no less a person than movies secret agent James Bond. When tackling the dastardly *Dr No*, in the film of that name, Bond sees the missing Goya on the arch villain's wall! For all the success there was in tracing it, it might well have been there.

In July 1962, Reuters received a second letter. 'The Duke is safe,' it said. His temperature was cared for, but his future was uncertain. Once again it demanded a ransom for charity, and once again a ransom was

refused. In December 1963, there was a third letter, suggesting that the major newspaper proprietors should pay a small tax on every 1,000 copies sold. Finally, in March 1965, the thief, clearly becoming frustrated, issued his 'fifth and final demand'. He offered to return the picture provided it was put on display for several weeks and the attendance fees given to charity. 'Liberty was risked in what I mistakenly thought was a magnificent gesture,' it ended sourly, 'all to no purpose so far.' Perhaps gambling on the assumption that such a literate and conscientious crook was unlikely to cause the painting lasting damage, the authorities still refused to comply.

In May 1965, a tall, nervous young man, who gave his name as Mr Bloxham, left a package at the left-luggage counter of Birmingham railroad station. Seventeen days later *The Daily Mirror* newspaper received an anonymous note which included a left-luggage ticket. When police went to collect the parcel, they found the missing Goya, deprived of its frame but otherwise in good condition.

Belated confession

And there the curious tale might have ended had the culprit not suddenly given himself up. Kempton Bunton, an unemployed truck driver from Newcastle upon Tyne, walked into Scotland Yard and confessed to having stolen the Goya. He described how he had entered the gallery up a ladder left near a back window by workmen. He had no particular need for the Goya — despite the fact that it had been acquired by the gallery only a few weeks before for $392,000. Any famous painting would have done. There were no guards around, so he took the picture and left the way he had come. Asked why he was confessing to the crime, he said that he felt sure someone was about to inform on him to claim the reward. He seemed confident that the police would not be able to prove criminal intent, and that without that he would not be convicted.

The trial began in November 1965 and lasted for 12 days. Bunton claimed that his motive had been to protest on behalf of old-age pensioners who, like everyone else in Britain, are required to pay a license fee for the use of a television set. He was able to produce

evidence of a history of protest in this cause. True enough, the prosecution was unable to prove criminal intent, and Bunton was acquitted on the charge of stealing the Goya. He was unable to account satisfactorily for the frame, however, and was sentenced to three months for the theft of that. And thus the mystery of the missing Duke was finally wrapped up.

Above:
In 1961, Goya's rich portrait of the Duke of Wellington was stolen from London's National Gallery. It remained missing for several years while the thief tried to ransom it back for charity.

Riviera follies

Above:
'Still Life with a teapot', one of the Cézannes stolen from the exhibition at the Pavillon de Vendôme, Aix-en-Provence, on 13th August 1961.

In 1892, the painter Paul Signac's boat was forced into the small harbor of St Tropez by a sudden squall. He immediately fell in love with the bay's sandy beaches and blue sea and skies, and St Tropez soon became a favorite haunt of France's bohemian community. Gradually it attracted the rich and famous from all over the world, until the Riviera and St Tropez in particular became the playground of Europe. In the 1960s, the Riviera was the scene of a spectacular series of art thefts which might have come straight from a glossy heist movie.

The first robberies to excite attention occurred at Villefranche and Menton. A wealthy Paris dealer, Armound Drouant, had a villa at Villefranche which housed some of his private collection. On the night of 11th January 1960, it was broken into and 30 paintings removed. The police were still struggling with the case when, two months later, the museum at Menton was robbed of seven paintings, including a Modigliani. Then, a week later, the Colombe d'Or at Saint-Paul-de-Vence was broken into, with the loss of more paintings.

The Colombe d'Or was an inn opened by Paul Roux in the 1920s. It was a great favorite among visiting artists who, if they couldn't pay their bills, found Roux accommodating enough to settle for a picture instead. In this way Roux built up a superb collection of early 20th-century paintings. When Roux died in 1955, his son took over the business and operated in the same way, undaunted by the fact that the value of his uninsured collection was mounting year by year. Then, on the night of 23rd March 1960, thieves broke into the Colombe d'Or and stripped it of 20 paintings valued at the time at $600,000, including several Braques, a Picasso, and works by Matisse and Modigliani.

The Riviera police, embarrassed by three crimes in a matter of months, were in a frenzy. In a manner worthy of Inspector Clouseau, they rounded up various suspects, interrogated them, but were forced to release them as innocent. On one occasion a suspect was followed by gendarmes disguised as nuns.

The thieves clearly did not intend their haul to be sold to shady dealers, for Roux received several ransom demands. The police kept secret the details of any negotiations, but on 14th February they received a phone call from someone claiming to be a priest, who told them to go to the baggage department at Marseilles station. There they were handed a large parcel containing 19 of Roux's paintings. But while excited observers were still wondering whether Roux had paid a ransom — rumored to be $20,000 — another, even more spectacular robbery took place.

In 1955, a millionaire named Georges Grammont died, leaving his collection of more than 100 Impressionist paintings and other objets d'art to St Tropez, with provision for a disused chapel to be set up as a gallery. Named the Museum of the Annunciation, it became the finest gallery on the Riviera, Dunoyer de Segonzac, the town's most respected resident painter, being appointed curator. On 15th July 1961 thieves used a key to enter via an outside gate, broke open an inside door, and carefully selected 57 of the collection's most important pieces, including two of Segonzac's own works. A tramp sleeping on a park bench nearby reported that he heard a Citroën drive off in the early hours, and a local resident complained about noisy revellers, but it was not until the arrival of the cleaning lady the next morning that the crime was discovered.

Segonzac was deeply upset, the museum authorities were appalled when they realized that the paintings were not insured against theft, and the police were beside themselves with frustration. Three weeks later the thieves struck again.

The raid at Aix

The town of Aix-en-Provence was having an exhibition devoted to the works of its most famous son, Paul Cézanne. It had been arranged by a Cézanne expert, Professor Novotny of Vienna, and included works loaned by the Louvre and individuals and institutions in America. In the light of the Riviera crimes, the Aix officials insisted on tight security. The grounds were patrolled by armed guards, and searchlights lit up the outside at night.

Some time between 1 o'clock and 4 o'clock in the morning on Sunday, 13th August, several men climbed a wall from a neighboring schoolyard and dropped down into the gallery's garden. They landed on a scattering of ripe mulberries fallen from an overhanging tree, and the juice stained their shoes, leaving a trail of purple footprints to mark their progress. They cut a wire which they assumed was connected to an alarm system (it wasn't, the gallery didn't have one), then one or two of them scaled the wall and entered through an open third-floor window. There was a guard in the building, but his room was on the first floor, and he heard nothing. A lady curator who lived on the third floor slept through the whole crime. The thieves took six Cézannes from the first room, abandoning a large portrait of the artist's father, which was too securely fastened to the wall, and then went up a further floor, taking two smaller pictures. All eight paintings, including 'The Artist's Sister' and one of the famous 'Card Players' series, were passed out and lowered from the window. The thieves made a clean getaway and the pictures were not discovered missing until the following morning.

With more than 60 pictures now missing, the French Minister of Cultural Affairs, André Malraux, intervened personally, exhorting the police to recover the pictures intact no matter what the cost. It was assumed that the same gang — said to be eight men operating from Marseilles — was responsible for all the thefts because the *modus operandi* was essentially the same. Both the St Tropez and Aix thefts were committed on public holiday weekends, the first on Bastille Day, the other on the Feast of the Assumption. There were the usual rumors: the crimes were a hoax; they had been carried out by an eccentric collector; they were committed by various sinister strangers. Two American art students were arrested carrying pictures at a railroad station, and it was several hours before they managed to convince the police that the pictures belonged to them.

By now, Segonzac had received the first ransom note for the St Tropez collection. The thieves demanded 50 million francs against a threat that the pictures would be destroyed. To prove that they were serious, the thieves sent a small piece cut from one of Segonzac's own watercolors. And with each demand they sent a further piece. Segonzac frantically tried to raise the ransom money from among his friends and admirers.

Picking up the pieces

The Cézanne paintings from Aix had been insured, however, and negotiations proceeded apace. From the insurers the thieves demanded 25 million francs. The police refused permission for the ransom to be paid, but in April 1962 they received a phone call directing them to a car abandoned in a Marseilles side street. For several hours the police watched the car, hoping to trap whoever had left it there, but had no luck. When they finally searched the car they found the eight Cézannes on the back seat, minus their frames. The pictures had to run one more risk, however, before being safely returned to Aix because the car taking them away broke down and burst into flames. Fortunately, the paintings were removed from the vehicle before any damage was done. It was widely rumored that a ransom had been paid.

Meanwhile, poor Segonzac was still negotiating for the return of the Annunciation collection. Unable to blackmail an insurance company or sell the pictures to a collector because they were too well known, the thieves were reduced to trying to raise what cash they could with guarantees of immunity from police prosecution. Segonzac offered to exchange one of his own pictures as part of the ransom, but his offer was not accepted. This was, perhaps, surprising, since whoever organized the crime was clearly interested in Segonzac.

In November 1962, the usual anonymous phone call told the police to look in a derelict barn outside the village of Villiers-Saint-George, 50 miles from Paris. Villiers-Saint-George was one of Segonzac's early haunts, and he painted several views of it. The paintings were found rolled up and hidden under heaps of straw. Some were slightly damaged by this treatment, but not seriously. Only one painting was still missing — the mutilated Segonzac watercolor.

The discovery of the paintings caused almost as much sensation as the robbery. Press and public demanded to know the details of behind-the-scenes maneuvering. Had a ransom

Left:
'The Card Players', another
of the Cézannes spirited
away from the exhibition in
Aix-en-Provence.

been paid? A curiously precise figure of $68,000 was mentioned. To what extent had André Malraux intervened? Had there been a deal? Would the crooks be prosecuted? Inevitably, the police issued bland assurances; the important fact was, after all, that the paintings had been recovered. But the strange story of the Riviera capers had one final twist. Gradually, the authorities began to return the pictures to their rightful owners, and the insurers who had already paid out for the Cézannes untangled the legal complications and reclaimed their money. 'The Artist's Sister' went back to the St Louis Art Museum in America. Before it was put back on display the museum's conservator embarked on a program of cleaning and restoring. While doing so, he noticed that the back of the canvas was coated with thick layers of glue apparently concealing paint. He slowly and carefully stripped them off, and found a portrait of an old peasant woman underneath — an early Cézanne the artist had abandoned before reusing the other side of the canvas. The museum had bought 'The Artist's Sister' for $7,500 in 1934; by the time they got it back from the Marseilles gang, rising prices and the second portrait had increased its value to $225,000!

The Marmottan theft

here were perhaps 30 foreign tourists in the Musée Marmottan on the morning of Sunday 27th October 1975. An elegant town house near the Bois de Boulogne in Paris, the museum had once been the home of Paul Marmottan, an art historian and collector. It housed one of the best collections of Impressionist paintings in France — over 50 by Claude Monet alone, with others by Renoir and Morisot, as well as furniture and treasures from the First Empire period. The priceless collection was protected by an expensive alarm system, connected to a local police station. It was, however, switched off during opening hours, since visitors had been known to trigger it accidentally.

At about 10 o'clock in the morning, five men double-parked their car outside the museum, calmly walked in through the main entrance, and carried out one of the most

Below:
The Marmottan Museum in Paris, once the home of wealthy collector Paul Marmottan, is now a gallery specializing in Impressionist works, particularly those of Monet. On Sunday 27th October 1985, thieves robbed the gallery at gunpoint, and stole nine priceless paintings.

sensational crimes in recent art history. Two of them produced guns and held up the tourists and attendants. The others studiously selected the paintings they wanted. Five Monets, two Renoirs, a Berthe Morisot and a Narusé were stolen, the Monets from the first floor, the others from rooms on the second floor. A glass case was carefully smashed open and the contents removed. 'They knew the layout of the museum perfectly, and knew exactly what

The first Impressionist painting

The theft was particularly stunning because it included the most famous Impressionist painting of them all, Monet's 'Impression Soleil Levant' ('Impression Sunrise'). A study of the waterfront at Le Havre, this rippling tableau of misty blues and oranges was first exhibited at the salon of the photographer Nadar in 1874. Painted in a much more expressive style than was the fashion of the day, it created such a

they wanted,' said an attendant. The thieves were in the building for little more than five minutes, and left through the front door, carrying the paintings with them. The pictures were put in the trunk, and the car drove off with the trunk open. In its planning and execution, the crime was breathtakingly simple. By the time the police arrived, the car was long gone. Nothing more has been heard of the pictures.

Above.

'Impression Sunrise' by Monet, the painting which gave its name to the Impressionist movement, was one of those stolen from the Musée Marmottan in Paris on 27th October 1985.

stir in the art world that one critic was prompted to say: 'Impression — I thought so... half-finished wallpaper is more finished than this sea-piece.' It was a comment which coined the term 'Impressionism', one of the richest, most innovative, and most influential movements in modern art. 'Impression Soleil Levant' is, therefore, rightly regarded as the first Impressionist painting.

Because it is so famous, it is impossible accurately to estimate the value, although the Marmottan's curator, the painter Yves Brayer, estimated shortly after the theft that it was worth 'at least 100 million francs' ($13 million). This is regarded as a conservative estimate; others have put it as high as $14 million. Nor were the other paintings financial lightweights — the Morisot had an estimated value of $1 million; the other Monets were put at between $175,000 and $280,000; and Narusé's portrait of Monet was worth $50,000.

The extreme fame of the pictures does not augur well for the thieves, however. As usual with the theft of particularly well-known paintings, it would be impossible to sell them on the black market, simply because they are too 'hot'. And in this case, the museum did not have its treasures insured — so the alternative method of cashing in on the crime, by holding the pictures to ransom, is unlikely to succeed.

Yet the thieves knew exactly which pictures they wanted, and were working to a plan which, though simple, was so thorough that it hardly seems likely they would not have made some plans for the disposal of the paintings. Since no demands have been made, at least in public, it seems improbable that they were motivated by politics or a desire for notoriety.

Perhaps this is one of those few cases where a wealthy, eccentric, covetous, and unprincipled collector might be behind it all, commissioning the theft of his favorite paintings for his exclusive appreciation.

Appendices

Right:
This cannon is part of the
wreckage of the French frigate
L'Herménie, *which went down*
off Bermuda in 1883. The islands
of the Caribbean are a treasure
hunter's paradise, offering
unrivaled opportunities for
underwater exploration.

I

Treasure hunting for all

Few people have the resources and opportunity to track down a lost treasure such as the *Nuestra Señora de Atocha* or the good fortune to stumble accidentally upon one like the Mildenhall silver. But diligent searching can reveal many old or not-so-old objects with both esthetic appeal and sometimes surprising value, and there is always a chance that, in seeking them, a true lost treasure may come to light. The hunt can add excitement to such mundane activities as clearing an attic or cellar, or even going to a garage sale.

By and large, we shall ignore the higher realms of antique collecting and fine art — expensive fields requiring considerable knowledge and experience, and full of pitfalls for the unwary — and concentrate instead on items that could lurk in the lumber room or be revealed in a weekend's amateur excavation.

Coins, tokens, and badges
Coins are the treasure hunter's quarry *par excellence*. They are durable, may possess both intrinsic and rarity value, and have a habit of being lost or forgotten. They have also been collectors' items for centuries, which carries two advantages: old collections often lie forgotten in dusty niches, possibly gaining considerably in value as they do so; and they are well cataloged, making it easy for anyone to check the significance of a find.

Any gold or silver coin is worth the intrinsic value of its precious metal content multiplied by its rarity value and, usually, its condition. High on the list according to all three categories is the uncirculated US Brasher doubloon of 1787, which would probably fetch $1 million or more on the market today. It is of gold, only about half a dozen examples are known, and, because it was not circulated, its condition is excellent. Copper, bronze, and cupro-nickel coins have little intrinsic value, but their rarity may command a high price. Just one example is known of the British George VI half-crown of 1952 and of the Elizabeth II penny of 1954, and the latter fetched some $30,000 when it was sold in 1978.

Tokens, issued in many countries by shops, taverns, and other establishments when small coin was scarce, are of base metal and usually low value, perhaps up to $100 in some cases. A curio among these items is a 19th-century replica of a Georgian British 'spade guinea' (itself a valuable coin), intended as a gambling chip. Badges range from military insignia to the emblems of medieval pilgrims and medals. Depending on the precious metal content

and rarity, some individual medals can be worth up to $75,000.

Stamps and notes

Stamps, banknotes, and related items such as stock certificates share many of the qualities of coins, although without intrinsic value or durability. Again, they have been collectors' items for a long time, so forgotten collections come to light relatively frequently; stamps also appear, of course, among hoards of letters or postcards. Probably the most famous rare stamp is the British Guiana 1c magenta of 1856, which is worth around $1 million, but there are others, such as the 5c US Blue Alexandria of 1846, worth as much or more. Misprinted sets of stamps are often valuable.

Ceramics and glass

Pottery remains are the most common items found in the excavation of both prehistoric and historic sites all around the world. Usually they occur as broken fragments or potsherds, but occasionally whole or slightly damaged objects are preserved. In most cases, these are of little monetary value; however, these are of enormous worth to archaeologists in establishing dates, cultural evolution, and trade patterns, so they should under no circumstances be treated lightly when seeking more appealing material.

Fine china and glass are a different story, and well-preserved early or rare examples can be worth a fortune. A single Meissen piece by J. J. Kaendler, the 18th-century modeler, may fetch $250,000. Chinese Ming porcelain found in quantity in an 18th-century shipwreck was provisionally valued at 'millions of dollars' in 1986; one Ming vase reached $600,000 at auction in 1974. A single Roman glass cup fetched more than $700,000 at auction in 1979.

Roman glass is not too likely to turn up outside museums and collections, but porcelain may well do so. Objects our great-grandparents

Above:
A vast collection of 17th-century pewterware has been recovered from the old pirates' base of Port Royal, near Kingston in Jamaica, now largely submerged beneath the Caribbean. Pewter is not intrinsically valuable, but these artifacts are priceless to archaeologists and historians for what they reveal of everyday life in the past.

bought for a few dollars have increased enormously in value over the past few years, in some cases by as much as twenty times their 1960s price. Of course, they must be genuine; pottery makers' marks are easy to forge reasonably convincingly. Worcester, Doulton, Derby, and Spode are some names to look for in 19th- and early 20th-century pottery and porcelain; in the 20th century, Wedgwood's

'Fairyland lustre' ware has become extremely valuable. In glass, 19th-century items from Boston & Sandwich and Mount Washington in the US, and from Nailsea in Britain, are now collector' items.

Of growing interest to collectors of limited means are 19th-century bottles and transfer-printed ceramic pots and jars. The bottles come in a whole range of exotic colors and shapes, while post-1840 pots may have colorfully printed lids and sides. Such items can often be found in pre-1900 garbage tips, and hunting them can be a cheap and rewarding way of learning something about basic excavation techniques (see Appendix III). Most of these bottles and pots are probably only worth up to about $30 each, but some rare examples can fetch between $4,000 and $5,000.

Weaponry

Primitive weaponry, such as stone or copper arrowheads and spearheads, is relatively common and not usually of high value. Collecting it was particularly fashionable among antiquarians of the 18th and 19th centuries, along with associated relics such as Indian war bonnets, and ready-made collections are frequently found. Deposits of primitive weapons unearthed when excavating a site should always be left undisturbed and immediately reported to a museum or professional archaeologist.

Daggers, swords, and firearms can vary enormously in value, but in very general terms those worth most date from the 16th century to the end of the 18th, when lavish decoration

with precious or semi-precious stones and gold or silver was almost compulsory among the well-to-do. At the top end of the scale, sale prices reach $200,000 or more. Handguns and rifles of the 19th and early 20th centuries are increasingly sought by collectors, and so are some later models such as the World War II German Luger.

Furniture

Louise XIV, Sheraton, Chippendale, and Hepplewhite are some of the magic names, but few of us are likely to stumble across them unawares, at least in the original; innumerable imitations are still being made. There is a growing market, however, for what might be called functional or country-style furniture, and that frequently comes to light, often camouflaged with layers of paint, in lumber rooms and barns. One of the most sought-after categories is the solid, plain Shaker style of the 18th and 19th centuries. Another is the British Arts and Crafts Movement, although later examples were sometimes mass-produced. Pre-1914 'furniture with a purpose', such as washstands, is increasingly valuable. A rarity in this category is the Virginia stool-shower with built-in back-scrubber of 1830.

By contrast, examples of early 20th-century Art Nouveau are now being eagerly hunted. Single chairs from recognized masters of the form can be worth $120,000.

Small items

In addition to the categories already mentioned, there are many other small items that have become recognized targets for collectors and therefore have a value well in excess of their original cost. Where they do not fall into an established class of antique ('antique' usually denotes something made before the turn of the present century; items after that period are often termed 'bygones'), they are sometimes called 'collectables'.

One of the widest ranges of small collectables can be labeled for convenience 'tools of the trade'. It embraces everything from early scientific instruments, such as astrolabes, microscopes, and telescopes, to bobbins and thimbles. Kitchen equipment is a popular sub-category, including corkscrews, various types of molds, and such rarities as American sorghum skimmers. Old fountain pens, inkwells, and blotters are also sought after.

Other functional items that many people collect include musical instruments, door furniture, coat hooks and stands, umbrellas, walking canes, pipes, cigarette cases, tobacco jars, purses, visiting-card holders...the list is virtually endless. Among non-functional objects to look out for are musical boxes, board games and pieces, toy soldiers and vehicles, and dolls and dolls' houses.

Assessing the finds

The first question most people ask upon finding a treasure is 'What's it worth?', even if they have no intention of selling. There are several sources to turn to for help.

One of the best, if the item seems particularly valuable, is an established auction house. Most of the major companies now offer a no-strings advisory service, including the price to expect at auction. Consult them on gold and silverware, jewelry, porcelain, fine art, and furniture, and perhaps on coins, stamps, and medals, old books, maps, and documents. With less valuable items in any of those categories, or collectables, auction houses prefer to deal with collections that can be sold as one lot.

Specialist dealers can also give an opinion. However, the valuation they put on objects amounts effectively to the price they are prepared to pay, and does not take account of their mark up when they sell.

Museums and archaeological societies can provide advice and assistance on the age and authenticity of objects, but are unlikely to commit themselves on the value, unless they themselves wish to acquire the find.

There are many books on antiques and other collectors' items. They can help in identifying a find, although it is difficult to relate an object to a two-dimensional picture or a written description. Use books as a preliminary check and then seek personal advice if the object appears valuable. Some catalogs – such as those for stamps and coins – include estimates of value, but these can be misleading and disappointing unless the accompanying notes are read carefully, as so much depends on condition. The literature on collectable bygones is sparser then that for recognized classes of antiques. In many cases, though. There are collectors' clubs and magazines to turn to for help.

Far left:
This bronze cannon, of French manufacture, was salvaged from the wreck of the Association *which went down off the Scilly Isles in 1707.*

Left:
A diver holding a jug recovered from the submerged city of Port Royal, Jamaica.

II

Law and the treasure hunter

The laws governing treasure hunting vary in their details around the world, but one basic principle holds true almost everywhere: other than on his own freehold property, the treasure hunter does not have any automatic right to pursue his quest. On leased or rented land, permission should be obtained in writing from the landlord (see below). Even on his own property he may not be automatically entitled to keep his finds. The same applies to treasure hunting in territorial waters. The position of wrecks in the open seas is more complicated, and has been the subject of lengthy lawsuits in the United States and Europe. However, several parties may have an overriding claim to a deepsea wreck — the navy of the country to which it belonged, the insurers, if they have met claims arising from it, the successors of the owners, and even salvage companies who may have taken the wreck in tow even though they subsequently lost it.

So before setting out on a treasure hunt, check the national or local laws carefully, and the procedures for reporting finds. Some countries insist that all items recovered must be reported to the public or to the national archaeological service, and that national museums have the first claim on them, with or without compensation for the finder. Many quite rightly impose restrictions on the export of antiquities.

Permission to explore a site should be obtained in advance, and is essential on privately owned or leased land. It should be in writing, and contain an agreement with the landowner on the division of any valuable items found, as well as on the mechanics of the exploration — such things as means of access, restoration of the site, and the time limit. The rules applicable to public land are more variable, but always with the proviso that the treasure hunter has no automatic right to explore them. Parks, commons, and village greens generally come under the aegis of the local council. Open land is generally administered by the state. River banks, river and lake beds, and foreshores may be privately owned or be the nominal property of a public authority; in America and Europe, restrictions are increasingly being placed on their exploration, even if they are public places. A permit is now required to excavate material from the foreshore of the River Thames in London, for example. The use of metal detectors may be subject to licensing and other restraints (see Appendix III)

In Anglo-Saxon law, the concept of 'treasure trove' often creates confusion. It applies to objects deliberately hidden by a previous owner with the apparent intention of returning to claim them later. By implication, the hiding place must, by its character, have some degree of permanence. Thus, a hole in the ground or a cavity in a house wall might be used to conceal treasure trove, but coins found in the pocket of antique clothing in an attic would probably not be classed in that category. In England, only articles containing gold or silver can be treasure trove; in Scotland and elsewhere, the definition is much wider. The decision as to whether a particular find is treasure trove or not is taken by a coroner or equivalent public official. The finder may receive the monetary value, or get the objects back if they are not wanted by a museum.

In addition to the legal requirements governing access to sites and the notification of finds, there are a few commonsense rules that responsible treasure hunters should observe.

Archaeological sites and ancient monuments should be left completely alone unless you are working with a recognized archaeological group. If you chance upon an archaeological site, report it to the local museum, and notify it of any unusual finds. Leave the site clean and tidy, filling in any holes before you go. Do not damage crops or frighten animals.

Finally, beware of lethal objects such as unexploded ammunition, bombs, or mines, and containers that may hold dangerous materials. Mark the spot, and report them immediately to the police.

Above:
The magnificent head of a granite statue of a pharaoh still in its original site at Luxor in Egypt.

Far left:
View from the southern gateway of the palace of Knossos, Crete. Knossos, the capital of the Bronze Age Minoan civilization, benefitted from the sensitive excavation techniques of Sir Arthur Evans (1851-1941).

III

Equipment and its uses

Right:
A diver using a camera attached to a grid to record the exact position of underwater finds.

Far right:
Inexpensive metal detectors have helped to make treasure hunting a hobby for many people. There are several different types, all of which can be mastered with a little practice. But in many parts of the world, there are laws governing both their technical specifications and where they may be used. It is always advisable to check these.

The high-tech paraphernalia of professional treasure hunters, particularly those who work underwater, is expensive. You can assemble a basic kit for use on land quite cheaply, and probably already own many of the items needed. Some of them can be used underwater too, but in addition you will need a diver's knife, a strong 'finds bag', underwater writing materials and a torch, and of course scuba diving equipment if you intend to work underwater for any length of time. No one should use scuba equipment without proper instruction and training beforehand; unaccompanied diving is dangerous. Before you dive, pay very careful attention to prevailing conditions — surface weather and winds, tides, currents, wave heights, water temperature, and underwater visibility.

Probably the most important item in any treasure hunter's kit is a trowel — not the rounded gardening type, but the kite-shaped kind with a pointed blade, used by bricklayers. In the hands of an experienced excavator, such a trowel is a precision instrument capable of removing delicate items from the ground without damage, and prising the top layers of dirt from them. Some people prefer a flat-bladed screwdriver for the same purpose. Underwater, the diver's knife can be used, with care. In very wet ground, a small hand-fork is sometimes better.

If the objects you are seeking lie fairly deep, remove the top layers of soil with an ordinary spade, or a fork if you are working on a garbage site. But make sure you switch to the trowel as you get lower down, so as not to damage any precious material. The depth of large objects, such as a chest or the foundations of a building, can be assessed beforehand by using a probe. An ordinary thin metal rod at least 2 ft long makes a suitable probe, but specialty stores sell more intricate versions with T-shaped handles and threaded points. Some also have a device for bringing up soil samples.

A hand-sieve is needed to sift soil or sand for small objects, such as coins or beads, that might otherwise be missed. If you use only one sieve, it should have a medium-coarse mesh. Professional archaeologists generally use several sieves in succession, with progressively finer meshes, to trace, for example, gems that have become separated from their mountings.

Polythene bags are essential for packing and removing small objects, and it is useful to have a haversack or some other large bag for carrying both equipment and finds. For serious treasure hunters, a map of the area, a compass, and a notebook for recording details of locations and objects are important, too. It is often useful to take a large ball of twine and pegs, to mark out the area being searched and to avoid covering the same ground twice by accident.

A further aid, for picking up small items of ferrous metal, is a powerful magnet. Marine magnets even enable you to explore shallow water without getting wet!

Metal detectors

The arrival on the market of relatively cheap and efficient metal detectors has stimulated many more people to take up treasure hunting as a hobby. Unfortunately, their indiscriminate and irresponsible use has excited the wrath of archaeologists, landowners, and conservationists, particularly in Europe. To some extent, this is being overcome by the formation of metal-detecting clubs that work closely with archaeologists and other experts to ensure that potentially important sites are not damaged or pillaged. In many countries, such as Britain, a license is needed to use a metal detector, and there are legal restrictions governing the frequencies on which they may be operated. In the United States, there are controls on the detector's electrical power output.

There are three types of detector, and all have their devotees, though none is capable of registering a large coin at depths of much more than 12 inches. The pulse induction (PI) detector is relatively insensitive to thin materials — an advantage if the object is merely a scrap of silver paper — and to the mild conduction effects that occur in wet soil or sand, which can be misleading to the operator. On the other hand, PIs tend to pick up ferrous metals, quite often worthless, at considerable depths, and cannot be satisfactorily tuned to distinguish between ferrous and non-ferrous metals. Induction balance (IB) and beat frequency oscillator (BFO) machines can be adjusted to make this distinction, or to reject the cupro-nickel used in modern 'silver' coins. They can also be tuned to filter out ground effects, and some IBs come with immediate reset buttons to adjust them for changes in the natural conductivity of the soil.

Eager digging that reveals only a beer can is an all-too-familiar experience for detector operators. It is an inevitable incident when using PI machines, and may happen with the other types even if they are set to distinguish between ferrous and non ferrous metals (most cans are predominantly tinplate over steel). Ring-pulls and can tops are aluminum, thus registering as non- ferrous. The machine has not been made that can tell the difference between a ring-pull and a gold ring of similar proportions. However, after some practice with a detector, the operator learns from its responses to judge the size and shape of underground objects, and also the variations in response that are often due to minor temperature fluctuations.

Cleaning the finds

The cleaning and restoring of ancient objects is a precise craft. In general, all you should do is remove as much of the soil as you safely can by gentle brushing; a soft toothbrush is useful in the final stages. Then, seek expert advice from a local museum, antique shop, or jeweler. Items made entirely of gold can be washed in warm, soapy water, but such treatment can damage other materials if, for example, the gold is part of a necklace. Marine encrustation on any valuable object should normally be removed by an expert. Organic materials, such as wood, leather, or textiles, found in water or waterlogged soil should be kept immersed in water from the site in a polythene bag or suitable container until cleaning by an expert can begin.

Far left:
Divers working on the wreck of an ancient merchant ship off Bodrum, on the coast of Turkey, carry baskets of recovered artifacts to a submerged decompression chamber in preparation for returning to the surface.

Below:
Off Kyrenia, on the coast of Cyprus, a diver uses an air saw to help him in excavating a wreck. Professional archaeologists can use such saws safely, but in amateur hands they can cause untold damage to valuable remains.

Left:
*The removal of accumulated sand
and silt is a major problem for
underwater excavators, but over the
past 40 years a number of devices
have been developed to do it. Here, an
air pump shifts sand from the remains
of* De Liefde *in the Shetland Isles.*

Index

*Page numbers in
italics refer to
illustrations*

Picture Credits

Michael Baigent 115 **Bridgeman Art Library** 58, 63, 126, 131 **Bridgeman Art Library - Dulwich Picture Gallery** 157 **Bridgeman Art Library - Kenwood House** 159, front jacket centre **Bridgeman Art Library - Musée d'Orsay** 168-169 **Bridgeman Art Library - Musée Marmottan** 170-171, 173 **Bridgeman Art Library - National Museum of Wales** 166 **British Museum** 122 top, 123 top, 127, 135 **J. Allan Cash Photolibrary** 24, 49, 112-113, 160-161 **Christie's Amsterdam** 32, 33, 34 **Bruce Coleman** 76 bottom, 77 left, 77 right **Sue Cunningham Photographic** 145 **Michael Dent** 28-29 **Diaf** 110-111 **C.M. Dixon** 89 right, 121 bottom **C.M. Dixon - Muzeul National de Istorie, Bucharest** 121 top **Mary Evans Picture Library** 64 top, 64 bottom, 84 **Florida Division of Archives, History & Records Department** 51 top, 51 bottom **Werner Forman Archive - Museum of the American Indian, Heye Foundation, New York** 89 left **Giraudon - Musée du Louvre** 114, 163 **Eric Hayes** 30-31 **photo © Michael Holford** 104-105 **photo © Michael Holford (Collection British Museum)** 73 left, 73 right, 90, 100, 102-103, 103, 155 **Hulton Picture Company** 9 top, 20 left, 65 top, 65 bottom, 72, 76 top, 152 **Robert Hunt Library** 52-53, 133 top, 133 bottom, 156 **Image Bank** 47, 86-87 **Kings Lynn & West Norfolk Borough Council** 130 **MacQuitty Collection** 2, 91 right, 93, 94-95, 98, 99, 181 **Magdalene College Library, Cambridge** 56 **Magyar Nemzeti Múzeum, Budapest** 158 **Mansell Collection** 16, 22, 23 bottom, 85, 128 top, 128 bottom, 136, 137 **Marion & Tony Morrison, South American Pictures** 69 bottom, 70, 71 top, 78 top, 78 bottom, 79 left, 79 right, 80, 81, 82, 83, 106, 107, 108, 109, 118, 119, back jacket **Multimedia Books** 20 centre, 20 right, 25 top, 25 bottom **The National Gallery, London, reproduced by courtesy of the Trustees** 165 **Peter Newark's Pictures** 7, 9 bottom, 10, 11, 12, 13, 14-15, 17, 18-19, 19, 21, 23 top, 42, 46 top, 50, 69 top, 71 bottom, 122 bottom, 148, 149, 150-151 **Photographers' Library** 183 **Photo Source** 26-27, 48, 101, 125, 138, 140, 164 **Planet Earth Pictures** 35, 38, 39, 40 left, 40 right, 43, 44, 45, 46 bottom, 57, 61, 62, 174-175, 177, 178 right, 182, 184, 185, 186-187, front jacket left **Popperfotos** 129, 142, 143, 144, 146, 147, 162 **Spectrum Colour Library** 59, 123 bottom, 124 **Frank Spooner - Gamma** 170 **Sunday Times - photo Ian Yeomans** 54, 55 **Woods Hole Oceanographic Institute** 66, 67 top, 67 bottom **Worlds Edge Picture Library** 60 top, 60 bottom, 178 left **ZEFA Picture Library** 1, 4-5, 36, 37, 41, 74, 75, 91 left, 92, 96, 97, 116-117, 132, 139, 141, 153, 180, front jacket right.

Multimedia Books Ltd have endeavoured to observe the legal requirements with regard to the rights of suppliers of photographic material.